THE PORTSMOUTH HARBOUR STORY

CROSSING THE HARBOUR

AN ILLUSTRATED HISTORY

Lesley Burton
and
Brian Musselwhite

HALSGROVE

First Published in Great Britain in 2000 by Halsgrove

British Library Cataloguing in Publication Data

Data for this publication is available from the British Library

ISBN 1 84114 088 0

HALSGROVE

Halsgrove House
Lower Moor Way
Tiverton
Devon EX16 6SS
Tel: 01884 243242
Fax 01884 243325
www.halsgrove.com

Printed and bound in Great Britain by
Hackman Printers Ltd, Rhondda

CONTENTS

ACKNOWLEDGEMENTS

In preparing this book we have a number of people to thank. They responded to our requests for invaluable research material, helped us identify the finer points of some of the photographs and, indeed, loaned us some of the superb photographs that you see in the book.

They are:

Elisa Wright, Marketing Executive, the Berkeley Festival Waterfront Co. Ltd.
Cheryl Nightingale, Secretary of the International Festival of the Sea Co. Ltd.
Charles Withinshaw of the Portsmouth Harbour Ferry Co. Ltd.
Lesley Frampton, Nikki Howard and Michael Nutt of Gosport Borough Council.
Janice Birkinshaw of Portsmouth City Council. Peter Davies of
Hampshire County Council.
Freda Alan-Williams, Brian Russell, Adrian Knight, Beryl, Chris and Nick Peacey.
Charles and James Musselwhite for the loan of materials and extra photographic work.
Peter Watson for the line sketches in the text.
The Staffs of Gosport Central Library – in particular Angela Gill – and
Gosport Museum.

To all of these people our heartfelt thanks again, for their enthusiastic co-operation and for showing such interest in the project.

Last, but by no means least, especial thanks to those people who readily offered their personal reminiscences, a number of which have been incorporated in the text and captions. Chief among these are the memories of Mr Arthur Dorey, whose specialist knowledge of the ferries spans half a century.

INTRODUCTION

Pause for a moment and absorb the special atmosphere of Portsmouth Harbour. Look at it in theatrical terms. The backdrop is Portsdown Hill, the great green barrier against all inland invaders, its part-chalk face gleaming in the morning sun. In the wings is Portchester Castle, one of the strongest of the surviving Roman forts in Britain. Across the water lies Whale Island, then the cranes, the masts and gantries of the Dockyard etched against the sky. The delicate rigging of the *Victory* seems almost to float above the surrounding boathouses and store sheds. Modern office blocks and a multi-storey car-park throw into dramatic relief the nineteenth-century shopfronts on the Hard. The white tower and cupola of St Thomas' Cathedral rise majestically over the rooftops of Old Portsmouth. Here lies the magnificently restored H.M.S. *Warrior* embodiment of the might of the Victorian Navy as she rides proudly at anchor close by the Hard. On the Gosport side, the squared-off diving tower of H.M.S. *Dolphin* and the sixteen-storey flats dominate the skyline. Seventeenth-century Holy Trinity, the oldest church within the Harbour communities, nestles between the protective tower blocks in a superb blend of the old and the new. Today a public house stands where the old Market House once dominated the end of the High Street – and latterly served as headquarters for the Hants and Dorset bus company. Who now remembers the 'Dive' café in its basement, the smoky den for off-duty bus drivers and conductors? But most dramatic of all is the Harbour mouth, with its centuries-old Round Tower on the Portsmouth side, matched by the Gosport sentinel of Fort Blockhouse. In time of the threat of war from France, 'a mightie Chaine of Iron' was stretched across the Harbour mouth. Inside the Harbour the inhabitants were safe, protected from the outside world. Portsmouth Harbour is the perfect sanctuary – it narrows to a mere 200 yards at its mouth. The Harbour is navigable at both high and low tides and its several creeks have provided anchorage throughout history for a bewildering variety of craft.

A more direct link between past and present is the bird-life of the Harbour. We may imagine that our forebears also watched the wheeling, squawking gulls and perhaps threw them scraps of food. For the prisoners once incarcerated within the rotting hulks, the seabirds must have symbolised freedom. Today the gulls provide entertainment for the tourist as they swoop for food in the wake of the passing ships or settle on the railings and seats of Gosport's Ferry Gardens.

Imagine you could step into a time-machine in Ferry Gardens. It takes us back to the year 501. Rumour has spread that the dreaded Saxons are approaching the coast. You watch nervously from the safety of the hidden gorse-fringed creeks as two large galleys rowed by sweating Saxons, under their commander Porth, enter the Harbour. They are encountered by Arthur, Commander-in-Chief of the Britons and his ally, Geraint-ab-Erbin. A bloody battle ensues. But the Britons are no match for the marauding Saxons. At last Porth reigns supreme. Eventually his sons, Beda and Megla, will settle on the western side of the Harbour, giving their names to the hamlets we know as Bedenham and Elson. It is said that a tumulus on Portsdown Hill marks the mass grave of the resisting Britons who made their last stand here against the all-conquering Saxons. Can it be then that the name 'Portsmouth' derives its origin from that Saxon leader Porth, or must we look even further back in time to the Romans who dubbed it 'Portus Magnus'?

The history of crossing the Harbour boasts a cast of thousands, from the lowly Briton ferrying himself across the water in his home-made coracle, to the most famous of our monarchs. Alfred, for example, sent out from the Harbour the first-ever fleet in order to engage the Danes in battle. King Harold gathered together his ships which were intended to oppose the landing of William the Conqueror. It is a roll-call of many of the most famous people in our history. But what would these folk from far-off days have thought of today's regular ferries, packed with passengers, mopeds, motor cycles and bikes? Here is our story of the Harbour, its crossings and its people, and how through the centuries they have come to terms with this piece of 'liquid history'.

INVADERS FROM OVER THE SEA

Centuries before Porth and his sons reached these shores, two great waterways dominated the South Hampshire landscape. In the long passage of time, the Solent and Spithead rivers merged and combined to form what we now know as the Solent. Its several sheltered harbours, including Portsmouth, are in effect drowned river valleys.

These prehistoric times are a dark and impenetrable labyrinth. Certain clues have come down to us – the great dried river beds yielded up hand axes, scraper tools, pieces of pottery, bronze and copper ornaments. All of this is clear evidence of the resourcefulness and skill of the early Harbour community people. But we can only guess at what daily life was like for the simple folk who vainly resisted the Saxon Porth. They were probably herdsmen and their sheep, cattle and goats roamed the thickly wooded land around the Harbour. Above them, the gentle slopes of Portsdown Hill afforded shelter from the overland

An ancient Briton in his coracle – possibly the first Harbour commuter!

Peter Watson

Portchester Castle, the oldest building within the Harbour and one of the marvels of the Roman occupation. This view shows the original Roman walls and bastions, and the church founded by Henry I as thanksgiving for his deliverance from the earthquake of 1133.

Portsmouth City Council

invaders but also provided fertile land for the cultivation of wheat and flax crops.

By the time we reach the year AD 500, the level of the sea had risen, vast stretches of the coastline were eroded and deep, silted channels formed in the upper reaches of the Harbour. Any invaders of this period would almost certainly have found the environment unattractive, leading them to look further inland or along the coast for a more well-disposed settlement to colonise. Visitors from over the seas were nevertheless very interested in the Harbour. In about the year AD 285, an enterprising Belgian sailor by the name of Carausius, who was appointed by the Romans, had sailed with his raiding party into Portsmouth Harbour intent upon conquest. He soon made the fortuitous discovery that the land beyond the Harbour rises somewhat above the preceding shallows and silted channels. Suitable land in fact for development and it was on this spot that Carausius built Portchester Castle, a huge and impressive piece of

military architecture with walls nearly ten feet thick and rising twenty feet over the low-lying marshes. We may wonder at the effect such a massive structure had upon the native population as they watched it rise above their own very simple wooden huts.

Marcus Aurelius Carausius is one of Roman Britain's most charismatic figures. He was appointed by the Emperor Maximian to rid the southern British coasts of the Saxon barbarians who, in their single open boats, were causing so much havoc to the Romano-British Emperor. Carausius was a first-class naval tactician – rare in a Roman conqueror – and his portrait appears on coins of the period as a stocky bulldog of a man. He was very ambitious – within a year or two of finishing Portchester Castle, he had himself proclaimed Emperor of Britain and ruled as such from Portchester until AD 293, when he was murdered by Allectus, his jealous Treasury official. Allectus was quite probably working under instructions from the Emperor Maximian, who may well have thought that Carausius needed taking down a peg or two! Be that as it may, Carausius' magnificent memorial has been bequeathed to us as the most splendid survival of the Roman occupation of Portsmouth Harbour.

Modern archaeological explorations at Portchester provide us with exciting clues as to the life of the people in the garrison. Remains of the bones of cattle, sheep and pigs suggest that animals were butchered on the spot for food. Vast quantities of oyster shells point to a regular consumption of the succulent mollusc which in Roman times was abundant in Portsmouth and Langstone Harbours.

Bracelets, brooches and hairpins as well as the remains of very young children indicate the presence of females in Portchester Castle. What was the lot of these garrison women, we may ask? Did they ever venture out into the Harbour or was life in this period too dangerous? Were they themselves virtual prisoners inside the Castle? We may never know, any more than we know for sure about life in Portchester Castle after the departure of Carausius.

The working life of the garrison is easier to imagine. Carausius' men were a commando-type unit, always at Action Stations ready for the Saxon menace whenever it appeared on the horizon.

From the Castle bastions, the inmates would have a superb view of the entire Harbour and particularly of its mouth. If you stand today on the top of Portsdown Hill and look down into the Harbour, it is not too difficult to visualize Carausius' men clambering into their shallow draught boats, axes and swords at the ready, when the warning bell is rung by the duty watchguard.

Little is known for certain of life at Portchester Castle after Carausius' departure, but by the fifth century the Saxon chief Porth was in command and it is entirely possible that he in turn made the Castle his garrison HQ. Archaeological finds again come to our aid – there is a wealth of Saxon material to support the case.

A Roman galley off Portchester Castle. Vessels like these would have been a common sight in the Harbour during Carausius' period as self-proclaimed 'Emperor of Britain'.

We go forward in time to the reign of Alfred when the greatest fear is from the north west in the shape of the dreaded Norsemen. Alfred – probably our first sailor king – built ships stronger and heavier than the invading Danes and Vikings and these revolutionary fleets went out from Portsmouth Harbour to engage the enemy at Spithead. During the period 985–1042, the south coast was invaded many times in spite of Alfred's well-trained seamen and technically superior fleet of ships.

In the first half of the eleventh century, the Godwines were the most powerful family in England, leaders of the national party against the growing Norman influence. When Edward the Confessor died in 1066, Earl Godwine's son Harold became king. His cross-Channel adversaries, the Normans, were in fact the descendants of those fierce Norsemen who had invaded these coasts three hundred years earlier. In the intervening period they had improved their image by settling in Northern France and becoming Christians.

They excelled in art, architecture and warfare and, again, their hungry eyes were trained on the southern coasts of Britain. Their leader was William, soon to assume the title of Conqueror, but not before Harold had put the fleet on the alert at Portsmouth in readiness for the expected invasion. Throughout the summer and autumn of 1066, the English fleet hung about the Harbour and Isle of Wight, using up its precious food supplies in the process. With no William in sight, Harold was forced to disperse his men and abandon the watch. He had been outmanoeuvred by William, who landed at Pevensey, defeated Harold at Hastings and brought about the Norman Conquest of Britain.

About sixty-seven years after the coming of William the Conqueror, a curious incident in the life of the Harbour took place. It clearly impressed those present at the time because historians of the period have described it in some detail. In the year 1133, Henry I was about to make his last expedition to France from the Harbour. We are told that – to the astonishment of the King's attendants – great clouds suddenly appeared in the sky and the sun disappeared behind them to re-emerge as bright as the moon. It became so dark that the Royal attendants were obliged to light candles although it was day.

Despite a calm sea and gentle breeze, the great anchors of one of the King's ships were moved by an 'unseen cause' so that all the fleet of ships drove into each other, eight ships in all being dashed to pieces. This is almost certainly an eye-

Portchester Castle's Norman Keep.

Portsmouth City Museums

witness account of an eclipse of the sun followed by an earth tremor. The resulting shock waves within the narrow confines must have indeed been terrifying. Minor earthquakes are not unknown in this area. In 1908, the citizens of Southsea were roused from their slumbers by some very frightening earth movements. In 1929, a large tremor was recorded just outside the Harbour, with its epicentre just beneath Spithead. Many people alive today will recall this particular incident. Henry I clearly regarded his tremor as an omen and in gratitude for his deliverance founded the church at Portchester.

It is only a few years after this event that the little community on the western flank of the Harbour got its name. Henry's successor, Stephen, was allegedly caught in a sudden storm at Spithead and was conveyed to a safe landing place by fishermen. Stephen's half-brother, Henry de Blois, Bishop of Winchester, granted this fishing village a charter allowing it to hold two fairs each year and three market days a week. Perhaps most interesting to us today is that he named this safe landing place God's Port. On the other side of the Harbour the fortified town of Portsmouth was growing in size and importance. In 1194, Richard Lionheart had returned there from the Crusades. Biding his time while his fleet was being re-equipped, Richard made a series of tours around the area, liked what he saw and granted Portsmouth its first charter, allowing its citizens to hold a fair each year lasting for fifteen days thus opening up the opportunity of trade with the King's French possessions.

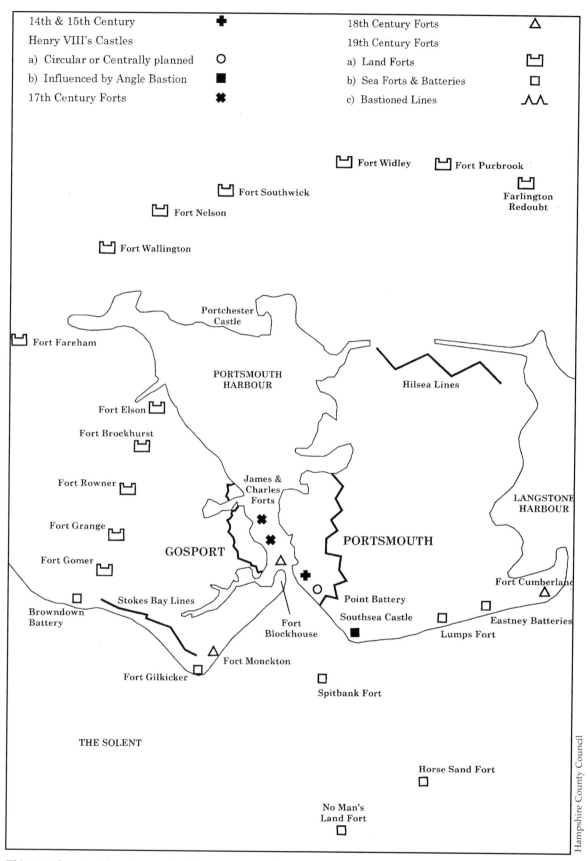

14th & 15th Century Henry VIII's Castles	✚	18th Century Forts	△
a) Circular or Centrally planned	○	19th Century Forts	
b) Influenced by Angle Bastion	■	a) Land Forts	⊔
17th Century Forts	✖	b) Sea Forts & Batteries	□
		c) Bastioned Lines	ᴧᴧ

Fort Widley

Fort Purbrook

Fort Southwick

Farlington Redoubt

Fort Nelson

Fort Wallington

Portchester Castle

Fort Fareham

PORTSMOUTH HARBOUR

Hilsea Lines

Fort Elson

Fort Brockhurst

Fort Rowner

James & Charles Forts

LANGSTONE HARBOUR

Fort Grange

GOSPORT

PORTSMOUTH

Fort Gomer

Fort Cumberland

Browndown Battery

Stokes Bay Lines

Point Battery

Southsea Castle

Eastney Batteries

Fort Blockhouse

Lumps Fort

Fort Gilkicker

Fort Monckton

Spitbank Fort

THE SOLENT

Horse Sand Fort

No Man's Land Fort

This map shows just how strongly the Harbour has been defended over the years by both land and sea.

Hampshire County Council

Chapter 2

ROW, ROW YOUR BOAT

Perhaps the single most important event to affect the life of the people of the Harbour communities was the development of the Royal Dockyard at Portsmouth. The Dockyard – pride and joy of successive monarchs from Alfred the Great onwards – fostered the trades and skills of the men of the area. The presence of the Dockyard embodied security for the nation as well as being the cradle of the south's shipbuilding industry. Furthermore, control of the Channel was vital if this country was to maintain its ascendency over France. Portsmouth Harbour, because of its sheltered position on the south coast, increasingly became the focus for the build-up of the Navy and, with it, England's maritime supremacy.

The Georgian storehouses and Semaphore Tower viewed from high on H.M.S. Victory.

An aerial view from 1972 of the Great Ship Basin of 1698, featuring H.M.S. Victory *in No. 2 Dry Dock.*

The Dockyard Main Gate in 1898, looking out on to the Hard.

A Victorian view of the Dockyard, showing storehouses and boatsheds.

The Main Gate of the Dockyard in 1904.

It was King John who, in the latter part of the thirteenth century, had begun the process of establishing dockyards within the Harbour. By 1497, Henry VII had presided over the greatly enlarged and sophisticated building programme for both the Dockyard and the strengthening of the Harbour fortifications. The rival port of Southampton had, since 1455, become the great commercial port of the south and would thus be unlikely to compete with Portsmouth in terms of naval superiority. Henry, it would appear, felt justified in pouring thousands of pounds into the strengthening of the Round Tower and the Blockhouse tower on the Gosport side of the Harbour mouth. These were now rebuilt in stone to replace the rotting wood of the earlier models. The 'mightie chaine' capable of stretching across the Harbour mouth was installed near the towers

At Southsea Castle, Henry VIII and his men watch the Mary Rose *sinking outside the Harbour in July 1545.*

Portsmouth City Museums

and would be put to use many times during the next three centuries in times of national tension. The Square Tower dates from this period and it is easy to imagine what a formidable aspect the towers, blockhouses and sea defences must have presented to enemy fleets. The French, nevertheless, were not deterred – in July 1545, their ships engaged the English Fleet at Spithead while, from the safety of Southsea Castle, an appalled Henry VIII watched in disbelief as the *Mary Rose* sank before his horrified gaze. Forty years or so later the people of the Harbour towns were again on the alert for the expected attack from the Spanish Armada. Men, ammunitions and provisions were rushed in to the Dockyard and surrounding fortifications, giving the ferrymen a tremendous boost in business as the community got itself ready for action. Beacons were lit on Portsdown Hill and in every town and village in Hampshire the people held their breath as they awaited the expected catastrophe. In fact, the English and

Spanish fleets engaged in battle off the Isle of Wight on 25 July 1588, when the Spanish fleet was scattered.

The Dockyard had assumed even greater national importance during Henry VIII's reign because of his several wars with France. Among the many great ships constructed here were the *Mary Rose* and the *Henry Grace à Dieu*. At over a thousand tons, the building of the *Grace à Dieu* involved the hiring of many hundreds of skilled men from the local communities when she was laid down in 1523. Shipwrights, sawyers, caulkers, pump-makers, smiths and carpenters were ensured of full employment in the magnificent new yard during the first half of the sixteenth century. This had a useful spin-off for the watermen, for all this labour force had to be conducted backwards and forwards across the Harbour. Gosport was a growing community at this time and, apart from fishing and agriculture, the people had some

One of the 85 ships built in the Dockyard during the reign of Henry VIII. A strong fleet enabled Henry to maintain naval supremacy over France and Spain.

Uncovering the 'mightie chaine'. Workmen in 1930 excavate the remains of the iron chain used to close off the mouth of the Harbour in the eighteenth century. The chain is thought to have been renewed by Henry Cort in his Gosport forge in 1785. Two links of the chain are now preserved in Southsea Castle Museum.

Gosport Museum Collection

expertise in boatbuilding skills. The local workforce was drawn in times of crisis to work in the King's great Dockyard at Portsmouth. A safe and reliable waterborne passage was therefore essential. Although crossing the Harbour in rough weather in a small rowing boat was hazardous to say the least, it was infinitely preferable – and safer! – than the long dangerous journey round to Portsmouth by land on almost non-existent roads with extensive patches of marshland. Here pirates and highwaymen lurked waiting to cut the throats of the unwary traveller. The wise workman therefore trusted his luck on the water. The boatmen would have to take account of the fact that stores, equipment and animals would be passengers on this ferry. There is enough evidence to suggest that a regular ferry service between Portsmouth and Gosport was operational from some time early in the sixteenth century.

The proof for the existence of this service can be found in a fascinating document dating from the year 1602 at the end of the reign of Elizabeth I. It seems that two men, Stephen Riddleson and John Jeffries of Gosport, had held the monopoly of the ferry crossing for some considerable time and for which they paid a rent to the Crown. Their management of this important little ferry service was challenged by three other Gosport residents,

Roger Trymlett, John Chesle and Erasmus Burgess. The Court of Exchequer at Southampton decided that Riddleson and Jeffries should bring the lease held by them to court to be cancelled by the Court and that Commissioners should be set up to look into the management of the ferry crossing between the two communities.

Suddenly we are back in the twenty-first century. How familiar it all seems! It is the age-old debate about monopolies and vested interests and the power wielded by a few individuals. But to return to Messrs. Riddleson and Jeffries – the Commissioners, having looked thoroughly into the case, concluded that no two individuals should ·hold a complete monopoly of this important and necessary ferry service. They recommended that the inhabitants of the borough of Gosport should furnish a convenient number of boats for the crossing of ordinary passengers as well as boats for the passage of troops and 'other necessities' for the relief of Portsmouth and the Isle of Wight. Twenty good and serviceable boats were to be always at the ready and that, for the transport of 'ordinary passengers' five boats should be made available, three for the use of horsemen, two for footmen and one boat at least to be continually on the other side of the Harbour next to Portsmouth so that passengers should not be

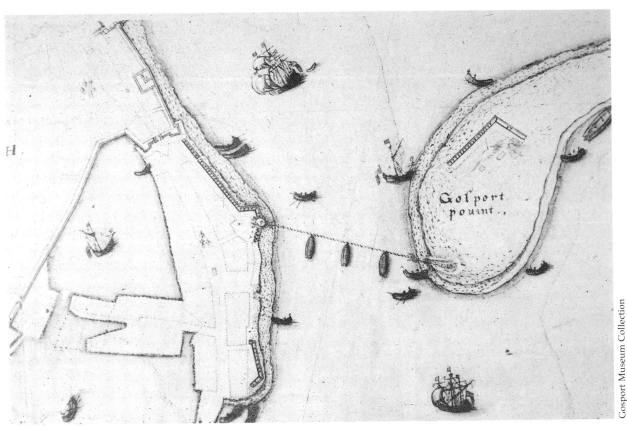

An early engraving – probably from the sixteenth century – of the entrance to the Harbour. Note the chain depicted as stretching across the Harbour mouth.

Gosport Museum Collection

delayed or hindered on their journey. For the safety of all types of passengers, the Commissioners recommended that two of the 'substantiallest' inhabitants of Gosport should be nominated each year and, with the constable of the day, should be responsible for the safety of the boats, the keeping of order and the regulating of the fares.

This astonishing document even details the scale of charges which faced the Elizabethan commuter. Every footman was charged one halfpenny to Portsmouth, one halfpenny for the fare back to Gosport 'and no more or greater sum to be paid by any person or persons'. Finally, the constable and the 'substantial' men should be responsible for the good conduct of the passengers and have the power to punish those who behaved in a disorderly manner against their fellow passengers. What Stephen Riddleson and John Jeffries thought of this new set-up has unfortunately not been recorded but the Harbour traffic had come a long way since the days of the early Briton in his coracle and the Roman commandoes in their flat-bottomed boats.

It was during this particular period that the local boatmen had an interesting involvement in the maintenance and repair of the Round Tower. All boats plying between the Harbour and the Isle of

Wight were required to bring a boatload of stones once a year and pile them against the Tower as a protection and a strengthening of the foundations. If this was not complied with, a fine of 2/- per boat was exacted. The Gosport ferrymen had to pay 1/- a year in lieu of supplying the protective stones.

Ferry travel – despite the Commissioners' recommendations – still had its hazards. This is one Lieutenant Hammond's account of a crossing by boat from Portsmouth to Hillhead in the year 1635. The Lieutenant had originally intended to land on the Isle of Wight but, as we shall see, circumstances dictated otherwise:

> I did commit myself to the blustring winds and rowling (sic) waves with my sea pilotts who were so unfit for that passage at that time that quickly both they and I began to be sicke thereof; for by that time they had rowed a mile, the Wind did soe rise and the waves did so toss us, that we made all speed possibly we could to the shore, which was not amisse, although those churlish drunken Sotts muttered; for what with the tempestuousnesse of the weather; that made the sea so boysterous and swelling; what with the unrulinesse of my horse; the smallnesse of the Boat and the lightheadednesse of my Rowers, it was wisdome to

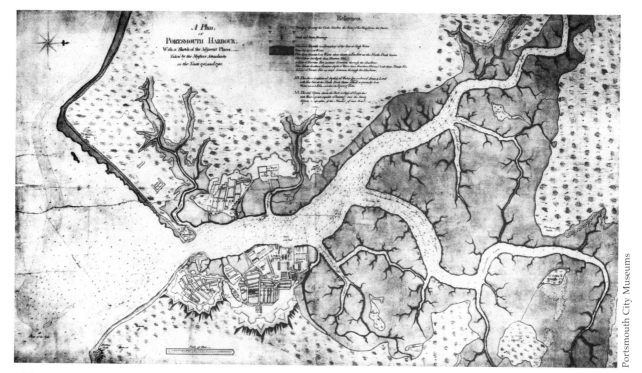

This 1784 plan of the Harbour shows the narrowness of the harbour entrance and the many creeks and inlets which provide safe anchorage. As can be seen, both Gosport and Portsmouth were heavily fortified at this time.

Portsmouth City Museums

Portsmouth City Council

The fortification at Old Portsmouth.

get off that great danger. And being soundly drenched with some difficulty we cast anchor with the quavering Beech and Sands where they left me betweene wind and weather to march 3 or 4 miles a desperate way to Hill Head, whither they could not but row me over till 10 of the clocks at night. In the interim, for that I must there spend my time and endanger myself, with a company of Sharkes that drinke like fishes and then have them along for my fellow travellers.

Anyone who has sailed this coastline in rough weather will surely sympathise with the queasy Lieutenant!

During the first years of Charles I's reign, the Dockyard suffered something of a decline. A political decision was taken to move shipbuilding nearer to London in the Thames Estuary at Gravesend, Deptford and Sheerness. No major works were undertaken at Portsmouth and it was not until Charles appointed his favourite, the Duke of Buckingham, to the post of Lord High Admiral that Portsmouth and the Harbour began to assume their former importance as the place where the big fleets came to rendezvous. This reached a climax in 1627, when a large fleet was sent out of the Harbour to relieve the French port of La Rochelle. The servicing of this expeditionary force gave work to the local craftsmen and plenty of business to the ferrymen. Unfortunately the expedition was a dismal failure and some 7000 disillusioned men returned to Portsmouth Harbour without payment for their endeavours and many of them were stricken with the plague into the bargain. Nemesis caught up with Buckingham in the shape of the assassin Felton while the country drifted slowly but inexorably towards civil war. As we shall see, a state of hostility existed between Portsmouth and Gosport during this period and its effects were considerable.

Chapter 3

CROSSING INTO ENEMY TERRITORY

The Harbour played an important part in the miserable Civil War which dragged on between the forces of King Charles and Parliament. Portsmouth itself was obviously a town of strategic importance, controlling as it did the entrance to the Harbour. Even in the months before the King raised his standard at Nottingham in August 1642 to signify the commencement of hostilities, the struggle for the possession of Portsmouth had begun. The Governor since 1639 had been the brave but untrustworthy Lord George Goring. In 1642, he was courted by both sides for some time before finally declaring allegiance to the King. Parliament, angry at what they considered to be Goring's treachery, and worried about the loss of such an important town, moved quickly and sent a large land force into the area under the command of Sir William Waller.

Most ordinary citizens here, as everywhere else in the kingdom, were indifferent to the power struggle as John Webb writes in *The Siege of Portsmouth in the Civil War*; it was as yet 'little more than an extension of the regular sporting activities of the country gentry'. But some citizens were forced into the struggle as Waller's men gathered recruits from Fareham, Gosport and Portchester in preparation for an attack on Portsmouth, while Goring looked for support from within the town itself. Tension mounted. Soon an incident occurred which was to draw Goring's attention to Gosport. Several supply carts containing wheat for the soldiers in the Portsmouth garrison were stopped and their contents confiscated by some Gosport watchmen

under the leadership of one 'Master Allyn'. Angered by the news, Goring threatened to bombard Gosport in retaliation until he was begged not to 'for the women and children's sake'. But his provocative stance had the effect of pushing most Gosport people firmly into the welcoming arms of the Parliamentary forces.

Thus, by late August 1642, to cross the Harbour was to pass into enemy territory! The rivalry between the towns quickly intensified. Along the beach on the Gosport side, men began to erect platforms. The work went on for a fortnight as the Portsmouth soldiers watched anxiously, noting with alarm that guns were being hauled up onto the platforms. While the Royalist soldiers were concentrating on this menacing development, a brilliant piece of opportunism gave their enemies a great success on the water. The pinnace, *Henrietta Maria*, was guarding the Harbour for the Royalists, with its six guns quite capable of inflicting considerable damage on the Parliamentary ships which lay a little way off. But one night, Lt Brown Bushell persuaded the Parliamentary captains to allow him to try a bold manoeuvre. Under cover of darkness, Bushell and some volunteers rowed longboats silently up to the pinnace, boarded and captured it without a shot being fired and gleefully sailed their 'prize', containing valuable food supplies as well as guns, away up the Harbour to Fareham.

Angered by this reverse, Goring ordered his men to fire across the Harbour, but a contemporary report claims that the Royalists' aim was poor:

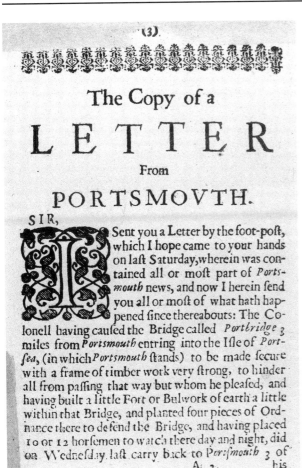

A document of the Civil War period referring to the defence of Portsmouth.

Portsmouth City Museums

losse to us (blessed be the Lord for it), no not of a man or horse'.

Now the Gosport gunners had their chance. On 2 September, the first shots were fired across at Portsmouth, killing one soldier and injuring another at Town Mount near Landport Gate. Quickly, the Royalists dug a trench on the Mount into which they might jump down in order to escape the bombardment. The next day, Gosport's attack was stronger. The gunners were ordered to aim at St Thomas's Church - a command that was not as sacreligious as it sounds, because the church-tower was being used by the defenders as a look-out. We learn that the Gosport gunners: 'played soundly... and shot through the Tower of the Church and brake one of the bells, and shot again against the said Tower, and that rebounded and fell into the Church, and shot down another top of a house that was near the Church, and the same Saturday morning they shot at the Water-mill, the Miller whereof commended it for a good thing to rise early in the morning, for (as he said) if he had not risen early that morning, he had been killed in his bed, for a bullet tooke away a sheete and part of his bed.'

As night fell on the Saturday, the Gosport guns provided a distraction to the anxious Portsmouth soldiers – it was part of a bold Parliamentary plan to finish off the Royalists once and for all. With Brown Bushell in command again, a number of foot soldiers were now able to scale the walls of the only other Royalists stronghold, Southsea Castle, singing psalms to keep up their spirits while the Gosport guns roared in the background. The Castle's commanding officer, Captain Challoner, was taken by surprise and forced to surrender. The Parliamentary invaders now turned the guns upon Portsmouth and fired a shot or two in that direction to let Goring know that the stronghold had been taken. The Governor apparently wanted to fight on, but the fall of the Castle and Gosport's accurate shooting had lowered morale and there was mass desertion from the Royalists ranks. Many said they would fight no more, fearing that the town would be 'battered down on all sides, and being frightened more by their wives!'

So Goring surrendered; he and his remaining loyal followers were allowed to leave and the Parliamentarians celebrated their victory. It was an important success so early in the war, and a bitter blow for King Charles. That was not quite the end of hostilities in this region, however. In January 1645, Goring, still in high command in the Royalist army despite his ignominious loss of

The Governour was much troubled, and presently shot at them, from all his workes, that lay that way-ward, letting fly that night at least 60 bullets, but hurt but one man therewith, and that by his owne folly, for he stood on his workes with a candle and lanthorne in his hand, whereby they had a right aime and so shot him.

Meanwhile, rumours and propaganda sheets circulated busily around the area. A huge Royalist force was supposed to be gathering near Romsey. Captain Wiles was said to have been killed by his own troops for changing his allegiance from Parliament to the King. No-one knew quite what to believe. But reality for the Royalists was that they were by now heavily besieged within the walls of Portsmouth. Such were the ways of war in those times that Waller and Goring actually dined together one evening as the Parliamentary leader attempted to arrange Portsmouth's surrender. But no agreement was reached - and the next day, 'they fell to it again, the Governour letting flie his Ordnance day and night, but not with any

Lord Goring, Royalist Governor of Portsmouth. A portrait by Van Dyke.

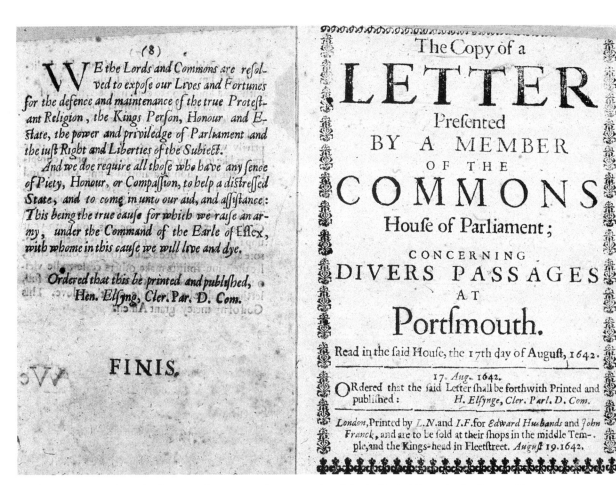

(8)

WE the Lords and Commons are resolved to expose our Lives and Fortunes for the defence and maintenance of the true Protestant Religion, the Kings Person, Honour and Estate, the power and priviledge of Parliament and the iust Right and Liberties of the Subiect.

And we doe require all those who have any sense of Piety, Honour, or Compassion, to help a distressed State, and to come in unto our aid, and assistance: This being the true cause for which we raise an army, under the Command of the Earle of Essex, with whome in this cause we will live and dye.

Ordered that this be printed and published,
Hen. Elsyng, Cler. Par. D. Com.

FINIS.

The Copy of a

LETTER

Presented

BY A MEMBER

OF THE

COMMONS

House of Parliament;

CONCERNING

DIVERS PASSAGES

AT

Portsmouth.

Read in the said House, the 17th day of August, 1642.

17. Aug. 1642.

ORdered that the said Letter shall be forthwith Printed and published: H. Elsynge, Cler. Parl. D. Com.

London, Printed by L.N. and I.F. for Edward Husbands and John Franck, and are to be sold at their shops in the middle Temple, and the Kings-head in Fleetstreet. August 19.1642.

Civil War propaganda – a leaflet urges the citizens of Portsmouth to join the Earl of Essex in the Cromwellian cause.

Portsmouth, returned with a large force to establish power in Romsey, Winchester and Salisbury. Recalling, no doubt, the part that Gosport had played in his defeat, he led a raid into the village. Twenty houses were burned down as panic-stricken people fled. Cattle, horses, sheep and personal possessions were stolen. A grim tale is told of the raid. One soldier trapped a wealthy citizen in his house and demanded this worthy's expensive finger rings. When the gentleman refused to give them up, the villainous soldier cut off two of this fingers to gain possession of the rings. Just to add to the confusion, Parliamentary ships in the Harbour under the command of Captain William Penn 'shot divers pieces of ordnance' at the raiders, but succeeded only in damaging more Gosport homes. Goring and his men made off with much booty, taking quite a few hostages with them.

It was a black day for Gosport but Parliament's victory in the war was not long delayed. Such, however, is the folly of war that less than twenty years later the feeble 'Commonwealth' had been totally discredited, the Monarchy restored, and crowds crossed the Harbour in peace and rejoiced to see the wedding of the restored King, Charles II, and Catherine of Braganza which took place at

Portsmouth on 27 May 1662. Among the onlookers was the diarist Evelyn, who described the arrival of the Portuguese princess and her train of ladies who wore 'monstrous fardingales, or guardinfantas; their complexions olivador and sufficiently disagreeable.' As for Catherine, 'she was yet of the handsomest countenance of all the rest, and, though low of stature, prettily shaped; languishing and excellent eyes; her teeth wronging her mouth by sticking a little too far out; for the rest, lovely enough.'

Did the shooting across the Harbour, limited as it was, leave behind something of a feeling of enmity between Portsmouth and Gosport?

The latter did resist its big brother's attempts to take it over during the next century. And in 1800 there was a significant little incident in the Harbour. The Mayor and Aldermen of Portsmouth set out across the Harbour to 'beat the bounds'; which, according to them, included all the creeks and inlets on the Gosport shore. But when they tried to land on the Gosport beaches, they were intercepted by large gangs of angry locals who threatened to duck the mayoral party if they dared set foot upon the shore.

Portsmouth City Museums

Catherine of Braganza, the bride of Charles II. Her arrival in Portsmouth Harbour in the spring of 1662 drew large crowds to see the Portuguese princess, who was described thus by the diarist John Evelyn: 'low of stature, prettily shaped, languishing and excellent eyes'.

Peter Watson

The Charles Royal, *the largest of the 26 ships built in the Dockyard between 1660 and 1685. Charles II visited the Dockyard when this vessel was under construction and declared himself 'infinitely pleased with the sight of the great new vessel for she would be the largest in England'.*

Chapter 4

A TRIP TO THE GIBBETS GENTLEMEN!

After the Civil War, the opposing sides licked their wounds and settled down to the business of making a living through trade, the manning of the Dockyard, shipbuilding and all the related maritime activities. In spite of the upheaval caused by the conflict between the two towns, work in the Dockyard continued. During the Protectorate period, Cromwell had reinforced the shipbuilding programme which culminated in the construction of the 468 ton frigate *Portsmouth*; duly launched in the Harbour in 1659.

After the Restoration, the boatyards of Portsmouth and Gosport flourished. Charles II – who had a lively interest in maritime affairs and was an accomplished sailor – encouraged the growth of yachting in the Harbour and this embryonic industry began on the Gosport side reaching pre-eminence nearly two centuries later in Camper and Nicholson's world-wide reputation for yachts of beauty, elegance and strength. Meanwhile, in the Dockyard another big shipbuilding programme got underway. Between 1660 and 1685, twenty-six vessels were laid down, bringing work to the artisans of the two communities.

An occasional interesting visitor to the locality was the diarist Samuel Pepys. Appointed Navy Secretary by Charles II, Pepys commuted regularly between London and Portsmouth to inspect the Dockyard and crossed to Gosport where the Commissioners for the Navy were keen to establish yards and bases useful to the Crown. Pepys – never a one to miss out on social activities – sampled the fashionable Portsmouth scene:

After dinner by water to the Yard. . . then we and our wives to see the *Mountagu*, which is a fine ship. And so to the toune again by water; and then did see the room where the Duke of Buckingham was killed by Felton. All our work was done, Sir G. Carteret, Sir W. Penn and I walked forth and I spied Mrs Pierce and another lady passing by, so I left them and went with the ladies and walked up and down and took them to Mrs Stephens and there give them wine and sweetmeats and were very happy.

It is unlikely that Pepys – or indeed any other officers on official business – used the services of watermen as such. More probably they would have used a barge supplied by the Admirality in much the same way that Dockyard staff today have the use of a special boat service. Charles II himself paid regular visits to Portsmouth to monitor the progress on the new strengthened fortifications for the Harbour. In 1683, he was accompanied by his Chief Engineer, Sir Bernard de Gomme. This visitation was marred by an unfortunate incident. As the Royal Yacht sailed through the Harbour entrance, the batteries of Fort Blockhouse fired a salute. Tragically, one of the guns exploded, killing the gunner.

The early years of the century saw the beginnings of the tourist industry in Portsmouth. It became fashionable to visit towns of interest and the Harbour figured high on the list of places to be seen. In 1728, Stephen Martin-Leake, a young clerk in the Navy Pay Office recorded his first impressions:

To view Portsmouth from Portsdown it

An early, relaxed version of Fort Blockhouse, c.1720.

Sir Bernard de Gomme, a Dutch-born engineer engaged by Charles II to strengthen the Harbour walls and defences.

Fort Blockhouse and Gilkicker Tower in 1729.

Bernard de Gomme's battery at Blockhouse Point in 1689. Across the water are the Round Tower, the Square Tower and the Cathedral.

The King's Bastion with the Spur Redoubt, part of the fortifications of Old Portsmouth. Jane Austen describes walks and airings on these ramparts in Mansfield Park.

Portsmouth City Museums

An oil painting from the early eighteenth century, showing the Saluting Platform, which was originally a gun platform erected to protect the approaches to the Harbour.

seems to be in the very water but when you come thither you are better reconciled to it ... there is but one church in the town, a very old building but it has a very good tower and chimes and in the upper part is a room where a man lives to give notice of all ships that appear off the Harbour, which he does by striking a bell as many times as there are ships.

This is almost certainly a reference to St Thomas' Cathedral whose tower – as in the Civil War – would have served as the perfect look-out post for the threat of approaching enemy ships.

Martin-Leake came to Portsmouth again the following year, mixing business with pleasure:

> I am at my old lodgings at Mrs. Waterman's where I have a neat clean room and furniture and there is a glass of as good French claret at the tavern for three shillings a bottle as ever I drank.

The club at Piles' Coffee House intrigued him:

> We have, wrote Stephen, 'clubs enough in London that deserve the name, never parting till early in the morning, but this don't meet till that time. . . their hour is four in the morning when they meet without disturbing the coffee people or their own families. The fire is laid in the coffee room and everything ready they may want overnight. He that comes first lets himself in, strikes a light, lights a fire and puts on the tea kettle. When so many are met, the coffee is made and after spending an hour drinking coffee, reading the news and talking politics, they separate.

Interesting to learn that Portsmouth folk were not wholly Dockyard-orientated and that coffee club society had percolated through to the South coast! Before we leave Stephen Martin-Leake, let's hear his opinion of the town over the water:

> . . . Gosport is a good town dependent upon the town and harbour of Portsmouth and therefore may be esteemed a part of it, as in common speech it is taken to be. It is much the pleasanter side to live on, having a fine country adjoining which you are in as soon as you go out of town; whereas from Portsmouth you must either cross the water, be confined to the Isle of Portsea, or ride five or six miles to come to a good country. Gosport is likewise esteemed a better situation and has good water in plenty, which Portsmouth wants. But then for company and agreeable living, Portsmouth is best. The garrison and corporation, the Navy, ordnance and dockyard and

Portsmouth Point – a lively engraving by Thomas Rowlandson which gives a good impression of local low life two hundred years ago.

This engraving suggests that sight-seeing in the Harbour was a popular pastime even a century-and-a-half ago. Note the number of female passengers in the wherries.

Portsmouth City Museums

Portsmouth City Museums

This is Rat Island, or, as sometimes known, Burrow Island. Once it housed convicts and in the seventeenth century was the site of Fort James which was built to help defend the Harbour.

the company that is brought thither by business or curiosity besides what the sea brings, naval or mercantile, makes as much difference almost between Portsmouth and Gosport as between town and country. Here are two good coffee houses, good taverns and the fold of business; there you have provisions something cheaper and some indeed prefer the air of Gosport; but they are so near akin I see no reason for it.

Reading this passage from a distance in time of two and a half centuries helps put into perspective the present day almost love-hate relationship between the rival communities forever locked in guardianship of the precious Harbour.

In 1739, another visitor, Joseph Yorke, the teenaged son of the Lord Chancellor Hardwicke, was taken for a sail from the Harbour out to Spithead as a birthday treat. Although it was August, young Joseph had a rough trip but, as we shall see, it did not prevent him from enjoying himself hugely:

> After breakfast we went on board the Commissioner's yacht. . . the wind and the tide being against us, the sea a little rough. . . I was never more nor indeed so much pleased with anything I ever saw before tho' mixed with bitter; for being a fresh water sailor I was a little sick but by the help of a little rum was soon recovered.

The eighteenth century saw England almost

continually at war with her Dutch, French and Spanish rivals in the race to colonise the underdeveloped world and capture the prized trade routes. Portsmouth Harbour was the focus for much of this ceaseless activity – here were gathered the merchants, the entrepreneurs, admirals, the men from the ministries and a rich and colourful low life. It was a heady mixture – this is the Reverend Dr James Bennett sounding off about Gosport in the year 1777:

> It has the narrowness and slander of a small country town without its rural simplicity and with a full share of the vices of Portsmouth, polluted by the fortunes of sailors and the extravagances of harlots.

In 1758, General James Wolfe had come to much the same conclusion about Portsmouth:

> The necessity of living in the midst of the diabolical citizens of Portsmouth is a real and unavoidable calamity. . . vice wears so ugly a garb that it disgusts rather than tempts.

Whatever else the two towns may have been, they were certainly not dull! It is tempting to imagine the scene as very like the celebrated 'Portsmouth Point' cartoon of Thomas Rowlandson. Here drunken sailors are fondling buxom barmaids while prostitutes and their pimps lure in the more able-bodied seamen, whose pockets are bulging with their prize money. In the Harbour, the sightseers are being rowed out to get a closer look at the great and

Quebec House, Old Portsmouth. In the eighteenth century, this building was the Customs House and is now a private resdence.

glorious 'wooden walls'; their full spinnakers echoing the voluptuous curves of the sailors' molls. Looking at the old prints of the time, it is possible to appreciate the somewhat seedy glamour that both Portsmouth and Gosport had in this period. There was certainly plenty for the curious to enjoy, especially those of a bloodthirsty turn of mind.

On a grey blustery March morning in the year 1757, Admiral John Byng was brought to His Majesty's ship *Monarch* in Portsmouth Harbour. Freshly shaved and smartly dressed in a light grey coat, white waistcoat with a fashionable large white wig, the Admiral was taken up on to the deck of the *Monarch*, where a firing squad of Marines awaited him. His crime, a so-called error of judgment against the French forces at Minorca during the Seven Years War, though probably Byng had been made a scapegoat for certain ministerial blunders. Let the reporter for the *Evening Post* set the scene for us:

> With the utmost difficulty and danger, it blowing a prodigious gale. . . it was most difficult to get up so high as the *Monarch* lay. Notwithstanding it blew so hard and the sea ran very high with great violence, there was a prodigious number of boats round the ship on the outside of the men o' war's boats, which kept off all the others. Not a soul was suffered to be on board *Monarch* except those belonging to the ship. But all the ships that lay near her were greatly crowded with spectators, all their shrouds and tops full, although it was difficult

to see anything on board the *Monarch*.

What some eagle-eyed spectator might have spotted was the bizarre sight of Byng's coffin being hoisted up on *Monarch's* deck at 7 am from a wherry, five hours before the Marines took their deadly aim.

In 1776, we were at war with America and there was much activity in and around the Harbour as ships were fitted out and seamen pressed in for the expected conflict. Skiffs, hoys, wherries and rowing boats covered the water surface conveying men, equipment and provisions to and from the Yard and the ships at anchor. Not everybody agreed with the war – one man felt so strongly about the injustice to the American colonists that he took appropriate action to register his disapproval. James Aitken had left his native Edinburgh to travel south on a secret mission to destroy the Dockyard's capacity to rearm against the rebellious colonists. He arrived in Portsmouth early in 1777, gained entry into the Dockyard and started a trail of fires, the most damaging of which was to the great Ropehouse.

Aitken is better known to us as 'Jack the Painter' one of his many aliases but which refers to the apprenticeship he served to a portrait painter. He was soon apprehended, tried at Winchester on 6 March 1777, found guilty and hanged at the Dockyard Gate from a gibbet over 60 feet high, fashioned from the mast of the *Arethusa*. After an hour, the corpse was removed and rowed over to

Admiral John Byng, Admiral of the Blue. Byng was executed by firing squad on board H.M.S. Monarch *in the Harbour in March 1767. Was he, perhaps, made a scapegoat for other men's blunders?*

Fort Blockhouse where it hung in chains as an awful warning to those with a treasonable frame of mind. Grim spectacles like these had a useful spinoff for the watermen. Many extra fares could be pocketed in ferrying the voyeuristic public across to Gosport to gaze at the rotting remains of miscreants like Aitken.

But it was a building at the mouth of the Harbour that attracted a quite different sort of sightseer. Haslar Hospital was begun in 1746 as a result of a policy decision by the Admiralty to try to stop sick sailors from absconding from their often sleazy and disease-ridden billets. The Admiralty correctly deduced that it would in the long run be more cost effective to invest in a large modern hospital than pay unscrupulous landlords to take in sick men via the 'contract' system. When Haslar Hospital was completed in about 1760, it was one of the largest brick buildings in Europe as well as being of revolutionary design for the period. Visiting monarchs made it a point of duty to inspect the Hospital. So did the composer Joseph Haydn in 1794. However, for reasons of 'national security' we were then at war with France – he was not allowed to visit the Dockyard which rather annoyed him: 'The Dockyard or the place where ships are built is of enormous size and has a great many splendid buildings. But I couldn't go there because I am a foreigner', he wrote in his diary.

The Royal Hospital, Haslar. This magnificent building was opened in 1756 and completed in 1760 and has been a familiar feature of the Gosport side of the Harbour ever since. At the time of its building, it was the largest brick-built construction in Europe. Now it faces an uncertain future.

For years, local convicts together with French prisoners-of-war were incarcerated in gloomy prison hulks in the middle of the Harbour. Here, the once-proud man-of-war H.M.S. York, *now reduced to a floating jail, is receiving another batch of prisoners. Many of them would spend a few years here before being transported to Australia.*

Because of the war with France and, on the principle that it is an ill wind which blows nobody any good, the 'locals' found plenty of opportunities for lining their pockets. The first run of French prisoners had been installed at Portchester Castle and Forton Prison on the Gosport side. These quickly became overcrowded and resort was had to the prison hulks up Harbour. The hulks were desolate, insanitary and rat-infested former ships of the line. Conditions on board were horrifying even for the eighteenth century. In 1786, a group of prisoners staged a protest against their degrading conditions inside one of the hulks and were gunned down by their guards, leaving eight dead and 36 severely wounded. As in the case of Aitken and Byng, so the watermen now cashed in on the Harbour presence of the French prisoners. A brisk sightseeing 'trade war' broke out between rival watermen, determined to satisfy the public's curiosity about the prisoners.

The Napoleonic Wars would test the capacity of another new building in the Harbour. Priddy's Hard – His Majesty's Royal Powder Magazine – had been finished in about 1770 and operational from 1777. It had owed its position on the Gosport side of the Harbour to the fact that the residents of the High Street and Broad Street in Portsmouth were terrified of fire and damage to their proper-

ties. Gunpowder was manufactured at the Gunwharf but stored in the Square Tower at the bottom of the High Street. Funerals – often conducted at night – passed from St Thomas' church close by the Square Tower and sometimes sparks struck from the iron carriage wheels, setting alight the straw laid down to deaden the sound of the cortège. The pitch from the link boys' torches was also a hazard – gunpowder could so easily be wafted along by the south-westerly wind and set alight. A massive explosion was a real possibility. There had in fact already been one near disaster and the aggrieved residents decided upon action. They raised a huge petition to George III to have the offensive gunpowder store removed from their midst. It is quite easy to identify with the problem. Nobody today for instance particularly wants to live next door to a nuclear power station! The petition was successful and in 1768, a new site at the mouth of Forton creek had been found for the powder magazine. From the moment it opened its doors as a going concern, Priddy's Hard had its own resident ferryman as well as its own small harbour and jetty, increasing even further the water activity in the upper reaches of the Harbour as gunpowder, ammunition and military stores were loaded on to hoys – small shallow draught sailing barges which took them out to the fleet at Spithead. Ammunition was not loaded on board in the Harbour because of

The Square and Round Towers in Broad Street, Portsmouth. In the early eighteenth century gunpowder was stored in the Square Tower, and after a number of explosions local citizens successfully petitioned George III to have the gunpowder removed to the Gosport side of the Harbour. This early version of 'not in my back yard' resulted in the beginning of 'Priddy's Hard' in Gosport.

the fear of explosions with the Dockyard so close across the water. A gunpowder explosion on board the *Marlborough* in 1776 had killed twelve men, three women and three children.

At about this time, the transfer of the Victualling Department from Portsmouth to Clarence Yard at Gosport was being organised where the estate in Weevil Lane offered the prospect of considerable redevelopment. The amount of beer, for example, consumed by His Britannic Majesty's sailors was such that an enlarged brewery was included in the Clarence Yard scheme. Beer was the livelihood of so many people on both sides of the Harbour and accounts for the enormous number of alehouses, taverns and inns of dubious reputation which mushroomed during the eighteenth century and gave both towns a world-wide – if notorious – reputation amongst seafarers. Like Priddy's Hard, Clarence Yard had its own watermen and a fleet of victualling hoys which were kept perpetually busy supplying the thirsty fleet.

Drinking and sightseeing apart, there were other types of entertainment to be sampled in the Harbour towns. The theatre was much enjoyed and at this particular time both Portsmouth and Gosport were full of sailors and the 'military' with

plenty of money in their pockets. Portsmouth's principal theatre in 1789 was in the High Street under the management of the actor Thomas Collins. Collins brought all the London stars to the town but there were frequently rowdy scenes in his theatre, the largely male audiences no doubt inflamed by all that beer. Over the water in Gosport, Henry Thornton was doing excellent business in his smart little theatre in Middle Street. He also captured the big 'names', one of whom was Mrs Dorothy Jordan, mistress of the Duke of Clarence, shortly to become William IV. Mrs Jordan was noted for her shapely legs and often appeared in transvestite roles to the delight of her male admirers.

Cross-Harbour rivalry between the two theatres reached fever pitch when Thornton put on a big 'spectacle' play by Richard Brinsley Sheridan entitled 'Pizarro' telling of the conquest of Peru. It played to full houses in Gosport and Collins quickly rehearsed the production for his High Street theatre. Too late, for the Portsmouth audience was crossing the water in droves to see the acclaimed Collins version at a cost of one penny on the ferry on fine nights! Wrote an aggrieved Thespian: 'Strange and mortifying that so small a town as Gosport should always boast of a better company'. Swallowing his professional pride, Collins closed

Gosport Museum Collection

The Gunpowder Magazine at Priddy's Hard.

Private Collection

Looking north, part of the great granary building on the quayside at Royal Clarence Yard which, together with the Royal William Yard at Plymouth, was for over 150 years one of the principal victualling suppliers for the forces.

Private Collection

Part of the slaughterhouse building at Royal Clarence Yard. The whole of this site is to undergo major redevelopment, but buildings such as this and the granary are considered to be of historical and architectural importance and will be retained as visitor attractions within the completed scheme.

his theatre for one evening and took his whole company over the water to see the Thornton version. Alas, when they took their seats it soon became apparent that the leading actor was the worse for drink and incapable of doing justice to the part.

Before we leave the leisure scene, mention must be made of another curious entertainment enjoyed by servicemen in the Harbour taverns. In the eighteenth century women wrestlers were often hired by alehouse keepers to amuse their customers. One of the most notorious of these women was 'Brandy Charlotte', a large and muscular but not unattractive woman. When an unfortunate Lieutenant of Marines attempted to trifle with her, she so laid about him that he almost lost the sight of one eye and had to be rescued by his fellow officers!

Portsmouth Harbour at the end of the eighteenth century was literally the gateway for a new life for many men and women. And not by any means a pleasant life; in 1787 the first shipment of convicts left the Harbour en route for Botany Bay in Australia. With the prospect of a thirty-six week voyage ahead of them, living in horribly cramped quarters with little to eat or drink, the mass misery of these unfortunates can be readily imagined. Problems, however, were just around the corner for the whole of the country and not just the Harbour towns, as we shall see.

THEATRE, GOSPORT.
BY DESIRE OF THE YOUNG GENTLEMEN
AT THE ACADEMY.
ON MONDAY, March 24, 1800, will be acted, for the First Time, a Comedy, called,
MANAGEMENT ;
OR, YOU TAKE THE HINT.
A favourite Dance by Mr. and Mrs. Ratchford.
To which will be added, a Musical Entertainment, called
THE PADLOCK.
On Tuesday, for the Twenty-second Time,
PIZARRO.
With a Farce, called
THE WEDDING DAY.
On Wednesday, for the First Time these Eighteen Years, a Comic Opera, called
THE MAID OF THE MILL.
With the Farce of
THE IRISHMAN IN LONDON.
And on Thursday, the Twenty-third Time,
PIZARRO.
With a Musical Piece, called
EMBARKATION ;
OR, THE RIVAL SOLDIERS.
N.B. A Waterman will attend at the Theatre Tavern each Night of Pizarro's being Performed.

The News, Portsmouth, Archives

This advertisement from the early 1800s in the Portsmouth Telegraph *proclaims that a waterman is ready to row theatregoers across to Portsmouth after the performance in Henry Thornton's Theatre in Gosport.*

SEA-BATHING.

AT FAREHAM, IN HAMPSHIRE.

THE TIDE, PERPETUAL, and WARM-BATHS, are open for the Season, and genteely attended. The situation is beautiful, and very retired, in a genteel neighbourhood, commanding extraordinary good roads to every part of the Kingdom; is nine miles from Portsmouth, and eleven from Southampton.

For particulars enquire of Mr. ENGLISH, Surgeon.

August 8, 1801.

The News, Portsmouth, Archives

The latest health fad in 1801 – elegant sea-bathing for gentlefolk in the upper reaches of the Harbour.

Portsmouth City Museums

An early nineteenth century view of the Harbour. The bathing machines on Southsea Beach contrast starkly with the gibbets and their unhappy victims over at Gosport at Fort Blockhouse!

Gosport Museum Collection

An early nineteenth century engraving shows turbulent seas in the Harbour.

With Gosport in the background, a flagship is firing a salute – but unfortunately the dignitaries being rowed in the barge are not known.

A fine engraving by Finden of the Harbour entrance, showing Fort Blockhouse.

Chapter 5

'MONOPILIZERS AND BAD MEN'

Now came the threat of an invasion from France and the long struggle of the Napoleonic Wars. Never before had Gosport and Portsmouth seen such hustle and bustle. There was plenty of employment for all, especially the wherrymen. There were over a thousand of them, busy ferrying passengers, naval stores and equipment around the Harbour to the anchored ships. As French prisoners-of-war were brought in and put aboard the hulks anchored in the Harbour, there was the opportunity to trade with them.

Off-duty sailors flocked to Gosport and Portsmouth to sample the delights offered by the dozens of taverns which clustered upon the shores. In 1800, there were ten inns on Beach Street alone in Gosport, including the long-lasting Isle of Wight Hoy which stood on the site now occupied by Crispins (and by a curious coincidence, one of the taverns a few yards along from that spot in 1800 was called The Old Crispin). Just as important to the pleasure-seeking seamen was the fact that females outnumbered males in the town by 14 to 10. As 'W.N.'; writing in the *Gentlemen's Monthly Magazine* in November 1802 so exquisitely explained,

> the Nymphs of the Sea, the Oceanides and Nereides of South-street and Rimes's-alley, form no inconsiderable portion of the number.

In Portsmouth, Dr George Pinckard observed the sailors' doings with amazement:

Poor Jack, with pockets full of prize money, or rich with the wages of a long and dangerous cruise, is instantly dragged (though, it must be confessed, not always against his consent) to a bagnio, or some filthy pot-house, where he is kept drinking, smoking, singing, dancing, swearing, and rioting, amidst one continual scene of debauchery, all day and all night... until his every farthing is gone. He is then left to sleep till he is sober, and awakes to return, pennyless, to his ship.

And, after this round of 'pleasure' was over, the canny wherrymen were ready to take the sailors back to their ships, often being able to charge quite exorbitant fares as their passengers suddenly remembered the penalties and punishments for being late!

Sometimes the boatmen could make money by bringing parties of women out to newly-returned men-o'-war for the gratification of the sailors on board. One seaman who served on the *Revenge* between 1805 and 1811 left an account of this practice, and described how

> a boat usually carried about ten of these poor creatures at a time, and will often bring off three cargoes of ladies in a day; so that if he is fortunate in his 'sales', as he calls them, he will make nearly five pounds by his three trips.

As the wars went on, more and more captured French ships were brought into the Harbour, to

On the foreshore at Gosport nearly two centuries ago, boys from Burney's Academy are among the sightseers impressed by the bustle in the Harbour.

A picture from The London Illustrated News *of mid-Victorian times shows convicts breaking up the hulk of the* York *by torchlight.*

Two rowing boats make their way in the Harbour in between an assortment of interesting vessels including H.M.S. Victory and H.M.S. Duke of Wellington. This photograph shows how busy the Harbour was in the 1880s.

the joy of the local populace, who were rowed out to see these prizes and jeer the prisoners as they were transferred to the hulks, which were soon teeming with these unfortunates. A picture painted in 1809 by one of the prisoners, Garneray, shows the Harbour so full of ships that it was a wonder there was any room for the wherrymen to find a pathway between them. Housewives, too, were reported to be crossing over to Portsmouth in large numbers to buy bread and meat, both of which were considerably cheaper over there at this time. There were nineteenth-century commuters, too:

> I also hear of journeymen working for masters at Gosport, and dwelling on the Portsmouth side of the water for greater cheapness of living

wrote 'W.N.'

In 1805, it seemed that everyone wanted to witness the departure of Nelson for the historic battle that was to prove so decisive in the war. Hundreds were rowed across the Harbour to join the throng outside the George Hotel. Nelson tried to avoid the crowd by taking the back entrance in Penny Street but the mob caught up with him on Southsea Common, wishing to shake his hand and wish him luck. 'I wish I had two hands,' the

great man is reputed to have remarked, 'then I could accommodate more of you' – and, as his boat left the beach, dozens waded into the water for one last handshake.

By 1809, complaints about over-charging by the watermen had grown to such a pitch that Gosport's authorities decided to draw up a table of fares and conditions. It was a long and complicated document. As far as most local travellers were concerned, the cross-Harbour rates were the most important:

IN FAIR WEATHER	s d
For one passenger, not exceeding eight, each	0 1
For a wherry for one passenger, not exceeding three	0 6
For four, not exceeding eight	0 8

In foul weather, the fares were 3d, 1/- and 1/6 respectively. Fortunately for the passengers, it was the ferry commissioners and not the boatmen who were allowed to decide what consititued fair or foul weather. Every possible destination was covered to hire a wherry from Gosport to Fareham cost 4/-, to Hardway 1/6, to the bathing machines at Southsea Common 1/-. Really tough watermen could make a lot of money if they were prepared to row across to the Isle of Wight – the

Crossing the Harbour in the 1890s. All modes of water transport can be seen – the steam launches, the wherries and, to the right, the Floating Bridge.

Gunboat Yard sheds and the 'Elephant' transporter in Haslar Creek.

An artist's impression of a peaceful scene outside the Dockyard gates in 1841. Often, however, in those days the area was notorious for quarrels, brawls and even murder.

Portsmouth City Museums

fare was 8/- to Brading or Cowes. The last section of the fare tarriff includes the fares for horses, mules and bullocks (2/-), and calves, sheep and hogs (3d) for a journey across the Harbour! By 1835, the fares had been revised; now three states of weather, fair, rough and foul, were specified, the prevailing conditions to be denoted by the flying of differentcoloured flags from the new Market House – a stately building that was to remain a familiar beach landmark until it was gutted by incendiary bombs in 1941.

The new Market House gazed down loftily upon bizarre comings and goings on Gosport beach. Dozens of watermen touted for trade amongst sorry cripples who had been discharged penniless from Haslar and were now reduced to begging. French prisoners of war from Forton jail hawked wares such as chessmen and ships made from beef-bones and dinner mats woven out of straw from their bedding. Local fishermen noisily advertised their morning's catch. On the other side of the water, respectable ladies and gentlemen tended to avoid Portsmouth Hard where robberies and drunkenness were daily occurrences. One angry man complained about a 'constant violation of public decency' on the Hard, where, he said, people had to witness every day:

> at least 50 persons, chiefly young men and boys, who are not content with having bathed,

but run about, naked, to an fro, in the public landing place.

Another nuisance in Portsea was the circulation of counterfeit money – including seven-shilling pieces – which had been manufactured cleverly by some of the French prisoners. Much local gossip and news concerned these men. It was rumoured that a waterman had been bribed to row one of them all the way to France. In 1813, there was great indignation when it was learned that eleven prisoners from the hulk *Vigilant* – hardly an appropriate name – had discovered some British sailors' uniforms, put them on, and then stolen the buoy boat reserved for the master attendant, whereupon they sailed out of the Harbour and eventually arrived in France! But any sneaking admiration some may have felt for these escapees was instantly dashed during the same year when a waterman named Brothers was stabbed to death in his boat by three French prisoners after he had refused to take them to their native land. At once, local watermen organised a collection for Brothers' family which raised £255, while the murderers were hanged at Winchester.

Just as some French prisoners were desperate to escape the hulks, there were also plenty of British sailors who could not cope with the primitive living conditions on our own ships. Two watermen, providing a stark contrast to Brothers' loyalty, were

Gosport Society Collection

The 'Grand Naval Review' of 1814, which took place in the presence of Tzar Alexander I of Russia, King Frederick William of Prussia, and the Prince Regent. This was the last Naval Review at which sailed vessels only took part – steam was soon to make its appearance.

convicted of aiding deserters from the Navy in June 1813. For this crime, they were themselves pressed into the service. Press-gangs were a notorious feature of local life at the time. Many of Gosport's alleys had iron gates across their narrow entrances to check the press-gangs, while at Portsmouth one escape way was via an inlet from the sea which passed under the bridge at Broad Street, whereby fugitives from the press-gangs could jump into the water and swim through to the Camber. But on one dreadful night, 500 Gosport men lost their liberty, according to the *Hampshire Telegraph*:

> At ten o' clock at night, Captain Bowen assembled a party of Marines, with as much noise as possible, to quell a pretended riot at Fort Monckton. . . as the news spread, crowds ran to the Fort and when the Captain saw he had obtained his object, he silently placed a party of Marines at the end of Haslar bridge, the only way out, and took every man who answered his purpose as he returned from the scene of the false alarm.

When peace came with the abdication of Napoleon in May 1814 (although of course he was to escape from Elba the next year to bring about

the events that culminated in the Battle of Waterloo) the news was celebrated by a special review of the fleet at Portsmouth, with Tzar Alexander and King William of Prussia as the guests of the Prince Regent. Gosport and Portsmouth were swelled with hundreds of visitors, providing watermen, tradesmen and lodging house keepers with plenty of cash. Flags and illuminations enlivened the streets and Haslar Hospital was honoured with a visit from the Tzar. Soon, however, hardship was to follow. The wars had been very costly and massive economies were introduced. There was a major reorganisation in the Dockyard, bringing severe cuts in the numbers of jobs. The Harbour scene became quieter. Boatmen and innkeepers did less business. Even the French prisoners had gone home, leaving the hulks to house local criminals instead. Later, these dismal floating wrecks were used to store strong gunpowder, sited as they were some distance from the shore in case of accident and later still, presumably smartened up somewhat, provided accommodation for sailors of the torpedo school H.M.S. *Vernon*. Frequent reports of desperate hardship appear in the *Hampshire Telegraph*. Charitable organisations such as the Dorcas Society did what they could. Some benevolent

An engraving of 1831 shows the bustling scene at what was then known as the 'Common Hard' at Portsmouth.

A review of troops on Southsea Common c. 1890. Clarence Pier is at the centre of the photograph and across the Harbour the distinctive water-tower of Haslar Hospital can be seen.

Gosport Museum Collection

H.M.S. Victory *at anchor close to Camper & Nicholson's boatyard on the Gosport side.*

gentlemen started up subscriptions for the poor, for, as one of these good people wrote in 1823, in Portsea:

> the relief afforded by the parish cannot be adequate to the actual wants, and many industrious and respectable poor families, in which there are five, six and seven children are at this time in very great distress and unable to procure needful food.

But life went on. Gradually, the nation's economy began to improve. The Admiralty's decision to transfer the victualling department for the Navy from King Street across the Harbour to Clarence Yard gave Gosport both prestige and work. The *Hampshire Telegraph* brought tit-bits of news relating to the Harbour. For instance, it reported in 1828, that a boat with a false bottom loaded with smuggled spirits had been seized by customs men off the Hard at Portsea. Before long, the vigilant men of the Custom-house were in action again, this time capturing 6 tons of tobacco from another vessel. The Hard at Portsea continued to provide the venue for a number of unpleasant arguments and incidents. There are many reports of fighting between soldiers and sailors. In July 1828, a serious row developed between a group of soldiers and some watermen over the payment of fares. During the fight, some soldiers drew their bayonets and several watermen received stab

wounds. Meanwhile, a new source of income had come the way of the wherrymen as visitors to the Harbour often asked to be rowed out to see the *Victory*, now in honourable retirement in the water near Gosport shore. But this service, and many others, had to be temporarily suspended on 9 March 1830, when a record low tide actually grounded the *Victory*, uncovered a large part of the Hamilton Bank, and, according to reports, enabled people to walk several hundred yards from South Parade out towards the Spit!

It was a tide of another kind – the tide of progress – that was to ultimately swamp the watermen. Inventors and engineers were beginning to realise the value of applying steam power to transport of all kinds. The Harbour had seen its first steamship in 1815, when the appearance of a 14 horse-power vessel had caused such a sensation that crowds had rushed to the waterfront and a courtmartial on board H.M.S. *Gladiator* had been suspended so that all could see the marvellous sight. In 1825, the first steam boat began regular runs to the Isle of Wight. But few could have predicted the appearance, in 1840, of a powerful, noisy monster that was to revolutionise the process of crossing the Harbour – the first floating bridge.

A vehicular ferry! What an exciting idea! Tradesmen and shopkeepers were delighted with the prospect. The Prospectus of the proposed com-

H.M.S. Victory, *here seen near the Gosport shore as a ferry boat approaches from Portsea, was soon to be removed from the water to undergo extensive restoration work, thus depriving watermen of one of their main resources of remuneration.*

Bessie Sinclair, wife of Henry Sinclair (manager of the Floating Bridge Company between 1894 and 1914) stands ready to welcome passengers at the Company's ticket office. The elegant structure, with its delicate ironwork on the roof, has been rendered even smarter by the gentleman on the stool who has just cleaned the windows.

pany made strong criticisms of the contemporary ways of crossing the Harbour:

> Injurious as this defective mode of communication is for Foot Passengers, the absence of any facility for general traffic is still more seriously felt – if a person living in Gosport

or its Neighbourhood wishes to visit, or to transact business in either Portsmouth or Portsea, by a Carriage or on Horseback, the circuit of the Harbour must be made,

it claimed. Interestingly, the vast majority of the 147 people who applied for the original shares lived in Portsmouth or Portsea. They included such worthies as coach proprietor Uriah Green, the engraver W. H. Charpentier and Mayor Hack. Gosportonians included innkeeper Thomas Hillman, brewer Benjamin Goodeve and clerk John Kempster Lipscount. On the board of directors were the influential J.P., Daniel Quarrier, Colonel Charles Menzies of the Royal Marines, and Sir Francis Austen, brother of the famous writer Jane Austen; and soon to join them was Robert Cruickshank, developer of the spa at Alverstoke and organiser of the new toll bridge at Haslar Creek.

To establish the floating bridge, the newly-formed Port of Portsmouth Floating Bridge Company had to obtain an Act of Parliament. At this stage, the watermen, realising that their livelihood was in danger, met together and produced this remarkable petition opposing the Bill, which they delivered to Lord Melbourne in Parliament in 1838:

> My Lord – The humble petition of eleven hundred Watermen who the greatest part have wifes and families to maintain and also as many House Holders – will use their prayer also for the Bill of the Floating Bridge that it may be thrown out of your Honourable House as it will be only feeding a very few Monopilizers and Bad Men to the

SUCCESS TO THE

WATERMEN

Of Portsmouth, Portsea, and Gosport.

Come all you jolly Watermen
  And listen to my song,
And if you will pay attention
  I'll not detain you long.
A set of Pen-born tyrants
  Have met, and they declare
That all our true-born Watermen
  A slavish badge shall wear.

CHORUS.

Then a groan for our oppressors,
  Who tyranny doth teach,
And a cheer for our jolly watermen
  That ply on Gosport beach.

Both hand and heart united
  We claim our ancient right,
With a full determination
  We'll not conquered be by might,
We use our best endeavours
  To gain the public approbation,
And with civility treat every fair
  No matter what their station.

On the first infringement of our wrong
  We made ourselves contented,
Tho to deprive us of our rights
  They a floating bridge invented.
They badged their men to scream and
  They wish we ne'er had met, [shout
But cheer up & sing the good old song
  "We may be happy yet."

You all know a man—I speak no names,
  Who at the present time supposes,
He can badge all our brave watermen
  Because he's got three noses,
He pokes them where he has no right—
  And as his nose so fast increases,
He'll run against a badge some night
  And smash his nose to pieces.

Now its currently reported
  That a very famous cadge,
Who sponges every waterman
  Is voting for the badge.
To Southsea common he'll be sent,
  So fast this cadging badger prated,
I'd give a crown with all my heart
  To see this badger baited.

They find the watermen combined,
  They've been so badly treated,
That they have quickly changed their
      mind
  And the Dutchman's been defeated.
The only badge that they will wear
  Is Friendships badge, together
With a long pull and a strong pull
  In calm or stormy weather.

The Watermen's Song. Thrown into panic at the prospect of the loss of their vested interests with the coming of the Floating Bridge, no doubt the watermen thrust this exaggerated and libellous piece of propaganda into the hands of their customers at every opportunity.

Portsmouth City Museums

The launch of an unknown warship in the Harbour c. 1830. The cheering crowds and fashionably-dressed ladies in the foreground suggest that this engraving was intended as a publicity exercise for the might of the British Navy.

Portsmouth City Museums

During the second half of the nineteenth century, shipbuilding in the Dockyard proceeded at a tremendous rate. Large crowds flocked to see launches, such as this one of H.M.S. Victoria in 1859. She was a powerful warship with 131 guns and engines capable of 1000 horse power.

ruin of Hundreds, this My Lord by your influence can be done away – as sent to the meeting of the United Watermen of Portsea, Portsmouth, Gosport and Hardway.

The petition, which also included some highly libellous comment concerning one or two of the directors, was signed by one John Mulhollen. And, as well as this appeal, the watermen also handed out to all their passengers a lively pamphlet.

The watermen met with no success. Most local people were enthralled at the idea of such an exciting novelty. The celebrated engineer, James Rendel, who had already been in charge of the installation of a floating bridge across the River Itchen, was appointed as chief engineer. The contract to build the first bridge went to Acraman's of Bristol who reckoned they could construct the vehicle and supply the requisite machinery and chains for £5900. Meanwhile work began by the local firm of McIntosh on the construction of the landing places at Point and Gosport Beach, watched by fascinated onlookers. The Clerk of Works, Mr John Deacon, who had been appointed by the company directors at a salary of two guineas a week, soon reported back that the work was going on 'with great vigour'. But there were snags. A visitor to the Portsmouth landing-stage site in 1839, Mr George Simson, wrote in his diary:

> Much difficulty having arisen in consequence of the shingles being so deep that they cannot, without a very heavy and unexpected expense, make the foundations – to the satisfaction of the watermen, many of whom will be thrown out of work when the Bridge is complete.

One can imagine the watermen's caustic comments and the irritation of the company workmen.

Because of these delays, and the fact that Acraman's in Bristol were taking much longer to build the bridge than had been anticipated, the opening of the new service was postponed again and again. The company meanwhile drew up its first list of tolls. Passengers could travel across for one penny, 'but if entering or using the Best Room or Cabin, 2d.' For a horse 'with coach, chariot, berlin, landau, phaeton, hearse, chaise, gig or cabriolet' the cost was 6d. Should you wish to transport a sheep across, you would have to pay ¾ d. for it, but oxen, bulls, heifers, 'dog drawing cart, unladen horse, mule or ass, rode or not rode', together with bath chairs, were rated at 3d. There were also rates for wheelbarrows, hand

The Dockyard entrance, 1855. The building to the left of the Main Gate still stands, and now serves as the Tourist Information Office.

Gosport Society Collection

One of the floating bridges at its Gosport base about a century ago.

Gosport Museum Collection

A cheerful figure from the past, now gone for ever. A waterman waits for custom in his boat with the eighteenth century houses of Beach Street – now also gone – behind him.

A superb Edwardian study of the floating bridge with one of the ferry company's landing stages in the foreground and
H.M.S. St Vincent *in the background.*

An engraving of the original floating bridge, emphasizing the elegance of her design. The bridges ceased running in 1959 after
nearly 120 years' service across the Harbour.

barrows and heavy waggons. This list, later to be amended, gives us a mental picture of the floating bridge as a veritable Noah's Ark.

In May 1839, the builders informed the company that:

> we shall, with extraordinary exertions, be able to complete the bridge by 10 July.

But the extraordinary exertions failed to do the trick and in November the directors reported that they

> lament exceedingly that they are not in a situation to report the arrival of the floating bridge from Bristol.

At last, in the spring of 1840, the bridge arrived, having been towed round from Bristol into the Harbour. As the company had lost money as a result of the delays, it was decided that there should be no special ceremonial opening. And so at noon on 4 May, the Harbour's first steam-powered ferry, packed with thrilled locals, made its stately way from Portsmouth to Gosport in twelve minutes, while glowering watermen watched at a safe distance, hoping in vain for a breakdown. The first travellers praised 'the smooth and noiseless operation' and soon the company's directors were reporting to their shareholders that the bridge:

is affording a convenience to the Public not before known in the neighbourhood and which is more highly estimated than any other Public Local Improvement made within the recollection of the oldest inhabitant.

During the first six months, the bridge catered for 220,000 passengers, 13,965 carriages, 3964 horses and 1763 cattle, as well as carrying the mail coach for London and other vehicles on their way from Portsmouth to link up with the L.S.W.R. station at Southampton.

Praise was heaped upon the new ferry system. The 1840 Guide Book to Portsmouth described it thus:

> This immense fabric is propelled by two steam engines of 16 horse-power each, and runs across the Harbour over two chains which have balance weights attached to either end so that in the roughest weather no motion is perceptible to those on board the Bridge.

The area near the Portsmouth terminal:

> assumed a gay appearance. . . gigs, flies, waggons, carts, horses passed and repassed to the delight of the residents there.

One of the floating bridges in 1856, crammed with sightseers for the Crimean War Victory Fleet Review. The artist has used considerable licence with regard to the size of the bridge! Note the watermen to the left, no doubt willing their mechanical monster enemy to break down.

Queen Victoria was an enthusiastic railway traveller. Here, at Gosport terminus station, she is handed down from her carriage by Louis Philippe of France, who was on a state visit to England which included trips to Gosport and Portsmouth. Prince Albert is behind the Queen in the carriage. From 1844, when the Royal couple purchased Osborne House in the Isle of Wight, they frequently used the station; from there, the Royal Train would be diverted into Clarence Yard whence they embarked for their island retreat.

Even better prospects were promised. The company directors reported excitedly that:

> they cannot overlook the amazing extension of traffic which must necessarily accrue to the Floating Bridge by the proposed Rail Road communication from Bishopstoke to Gosport, an Act of Parliament for establishing which has lately been obtained. . . it will ultimately answer the most sanguine expectations of the proprietors.

The railway duly arrived in 1842, causing increased traffic on the bridge and through the streets of Gosport, as Portsmouth still had no railway at this time.

Thus in a very short period of time, this area had become equipped with the very latest transport facilities that technology could achieve. Society, however, was slower to adapt to 'modern times'. The atrocious state of the back streets and crowded courtyards, poorly drained and seldom repaired, brought regular outbreaks of cholera and similar diseases on both sides of the Harbour. During the deadly cholera plague of 1849, bodies were brought over on the bridge to be buried at Browndown, so many and quick were the deaths in Portsea, while Gosport's streets were whitewashed

in the hope of reducing the disease. Criminals were still being transported to the colonies for certain offences. The *Hampshire Telegraph* meanwhile despaired of local morals:

> There are few towns in England having an equal population where the system of harbouring prostitutes in public houses is carried on to a greater extent than it is in Portsmouth.

The area, too, was to witness the last duel to be fought in England. The participants, Lt Hawkey of the Royal Marines and Capt. Seton of the 11th Dragoons, had quarrelled in the King's Rooms at Southsea, and the duel took place at Browndown where Seton was mortally wounded. It is amazing to think that these perpetrators of a barbaric old custom may have travelled across the Harbour for their duel on the floating bridge, the epitome of modern science and reason!

While the floating bridges (the company added a back-up one in 1842) clanked and puffed inexorably across the water, the wherrymen had to do the best they could to eke out a living. They could, of course, still handle the business of taking sailors to and from their ships, besides rowing passengers to the various spots round the coast outside the bridges' limits. One event in their favour was the opening, in 1847, of the Albert Pier at Portsea – a 1200-foot long wooden structure which enabled boats to be landed at all states of the tide. At this time too, Portsmouth was at last able to boast its own railway service – and this meant some loss of traffic for the floating bridge. But a big event in 1856 proved profitable to both watermen and the floating bridge company.

The visit of Queen Victoria to review the fleet after Britain's success in the Crimean War was an historic event. An estimated 100,000 people thronged the shores of the Harbour, including visitors from all over the country together with excursionists from France, Germany and Austria. Some sightseers, unable to get accommodation or afford the exorbitant prices being charged, spent the night before the review sleeping outside or leaning against chimney corners. Both floating bridges, by now bearing the names *Victoria* and *Albert*, were used as grandstands for the day, and even the watermen were hard-pressed to row the multitudes round the 254-strong fleet.

The floating bridges prospered through the fifties and sixties. Ever anxious to be in the vanguard of progress, the company introduced gas lighting to the *Albert* in 1859 via a small gasholder which was filled once a day from the supply pipe at Gosport shore. By 1864, the original bridge *Victoria* was becoming worn-out and she was replaced by *Alexandra*. Who would have imagined, watching this new bridge on her first travels, that she would still be running to and fro ninety-six years later?

Notable visitors to the Harbour at this time included the painter J.M.W. Turner and the writer W.S. Gilbert. Turner, who loved machinery and all things up-to-date, was fascinated by the workings of the floating bridge. In his diary, he described the complicated machinery, noting that 'it is a large, flat-bottomed boat, similar to the busses of the Middle Ages. The deck is covered with road-stuff so that carriages drive on board the same as it were a continuation of the road itself.' Gilbert, however, much preferred the old ways. A boatman rowed him round the Harbour and then up to *Victory* so that he could gather information and atmosphere for his meticulous setting of *H.M.S. Pinafore*.

But a change was coming. At the end of the 1860s, some enterprising watermen began to acquire little steam launches of their own. The smoke from the tall funnels produced the first faint clouds in the sky which up till now had been all clear for the floating bridge.

Gosport's 'smart set' gathered at Fort Monckton to see Queen Victoria review her fleet at the end of the Crimean War. Contemporary reports claimed that over half a million people witnessed the celebrations in Spithead.

Gosport Society Collection

An Edwardian postcard, depicting the Victory Anchor and Clarence Pier.

A superb photograph of the Hard in the 1890s, featuring among others the 'Harbour View' coffee tavern and the 'Queens Head'.

Chapter 6

FULL STEAM AHEAD

The new little steam launches were more versatile and nippy than the floating bridge. They were very much in evidence when in November 1869, many sightseers crowded onto them to take up advantageous positions to witness the launching from the Dockyard of the hull of the first ironclad ship, H.M.S. *Devastation*. The floating bridge company quickly rose to meet the new challenge. The directors reported in the following year that they:

> think it well to make introduction of a new accommodation for foot passengers by steam launches

and, in 1871, the first one duly appeared. She was a tiny boat called *Florence* and, so successful was she in claiming back some of the foot passengers, that the company ordered two more vessels of similar style. *Eva Mary* and *Sappho*. By 1874, profits were booming again. Individual launches, it seemed, just could not compete with the well organised company.

So, as their income dwindled away, a group of enterprising watermen decided 'if you can't beat 'em, join 'em.' After a meeting in Gosport, in 1875, came the news of the formation of the 'Gosport and Portsea Watermen's Steam Launch Company'; with the promise of a service every bit as regular as that of the floating bridge company's launches. A stroke of good fortune at once attended the newly formed company. In 1876, Portsmouth Harbour station was constructed as the London railway service was belatedly extended from the Town station, mainly to provide a link with the Isle of Wight ferries, the island having become increasingly popular thanks to the Queen's frequent visits there. Part of the condi-

tions of the Act of Parliament which allowed the railway extension demanded that a gangway and pier leading to a free public landing stage must be provided. Thus, the new company could run their service from Gosport Hard to the new landing stage, giving Gosport passengers the happy opportunity to use the new direct link-up railway service to London. And so the new service began. The first six boats of the new company – *Lily*, *Grand Duchess*, *Marquis of Lorne*, *Princess Louise*, *Elfin* and *Frances* – were all acquired from individual watermen in return for shares in the company.

The new Portsmouth Harbour station, the development of Commercial Road with its large shops and increased activity in the Dockyard in the 1880s combined to swell the number of regular users of the ferries. The increased traffic was reflected in the establishment on both sides of the Harbour of horse-drawn tram services. A horse-bus had run from Gosport railway station to the floating bridge terminal since 1859, but in 1882 the Gosport Tramways Company, under the aegis of the 'Provincial' firm, ran its first service along the newly-laid lines from Gosport Hard through Clarence Road, to reach Ann's Hill via Camdentown. Other routes soon followed.

It was not long before some of the remaining watermen met at Portsea to form a rival organisation to the other two. This was named the 'Port of Portsmouth Steam Launch and Towing Company'. To the annoyance of the Gosport Watermen's company, the new service also ran between Gosport Hard and the pontoon at Harbour station, but it also offered towing facilities for sailing ships and barges in and out of the Harbour. So the scene was set for a three-cornered struggle for passengers.

H.M.S. St Vincent *in the Harbour. She became a boys' training ship.*

H.M.S. St Vincent, *with Fort Blockhouse to the left and Gosport foreshore to the right.*

Private Collection

A fine late Victorian view of H.M.S. St Vincent and the training brig Martin at anchor in the Harbour. Between the vessels, on the Gosport shore may be seen the Old Market House, Camper & Nicholson's and Ratsey & Lapthorn.

Tate Gallery, London

'The Gallery on H.M.S. Calcutta', at Portsmouth, c.1876. A painting by James Tissot.

H.M.S. St Vincent. *This famous and much-loved 'wooden wall' was used as a training ship for boys and for many years was moored on the Gosport side of the Harbour. The regime on board was strict; the need for discipline and selfless attentiveness to duty was instilled in the minds of the youthful mariners. Locals used to enjoy watching the young trainees manning the yards, as they are in this photograph.*

Portsmouth City Museums

Portsmouth City Museums

This is Frances, *one of the Gosport & Portsea Watermen's Steam Launch Company's ferry boats which began service in 1878. A number of sailors mingle with other passengers as the launch approaches Gosport, while ladies in the stern are protecting their hats from the light rain.*

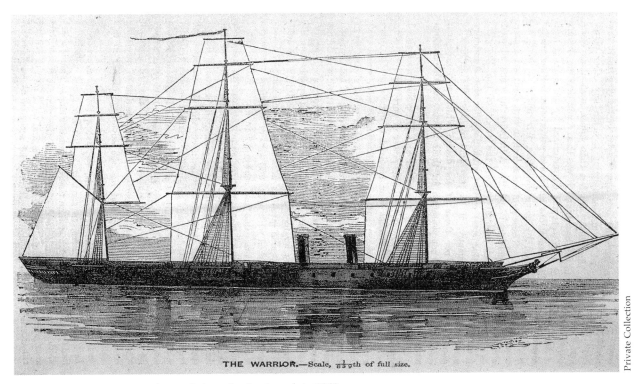

THE WARRIOR.—Scale, $\frac{1}{639}$th of full size.

Private Collection

H.M.S. Warrior *– an engraving made just after her launch in 1860.*

Portsmouth City Council

H.M.S. Warrior, *splendidly restored, resting alongside the Naval Base, her home since 1987.*

The paddle steamer Duchess of Edinburgh *decked out for a naval review. Built for the Joint Railways Fleet in 1886, she was a prominent sight in the Harbour until being scrapped in 1910.*

At Gosport, horse-drawn vehicles of several types await the arrival of one of the floating bridges. The older bridge is at stand-by, while the Company's offices and machine-housing buildings add a touch of elegance to this picture of a century ago.

Gosport Hard a century ago, showing both ferry companies' piers and ferries, with one of the floating bridges in the background.

At low tide, people stroll along one of the ferry piers at Gosport, while three smartly-dressed boys eye the camera. Note the heavy protection around the base of the elegant lamp; this was needed at high tides, as the lamps' bases were well under water.

Sailors gather near a single-decker horse tram at Gosport Hard in the early 1900s. The ferry office advertises fares of one halfpenny to cross the Harbour, and three halfpence for a bicycle and rider.

Photographs give us a fascinating view of the bustle of a century ago in the Harbour. There were vessels of every shape and size. Modern steam boats mingled with sailing ships while the floating bridge clanked to and fro under the lofty gaze of those picturesque veterans at anchor, *Victory* and *St Vincent*. The beach at Gosport presented a busy but higgledy-piggledy appearance, with its mixture of stone slipways, pontoons, advertising hoardings, a few gas lamps whose bases were sometimes under water at high tide, and the companies' offices and buildings arranged in various positions.

On the other side, the new pier and pontoon rovided an entrance to Portsmouth for ferry passengers at a spot which had for a long time been one of the most notorious areas of the town. Unpleasant incidents at the Hard and in the nearby streets were rife. In 1851, the *Hampshire Telegraph* had drawn attention to the nuisance of fruit-boys hawking their wares to Dockyardmen on the Hard at lunch-time, and the newspaper also criticised the habit of the workers hanging around the Hard:

Persons going along the Hard find it a very difficult matter to do so with any degree of comfort; and when it is remembered that about every other man has a short pipe in his mouth, in full and vigorous play, the thing is not merely – particularly to females – a discomfort, but a highly distasteful affair.

In the 1860s, there were complaints that seamen were frequently brawling outside the area's many taverns:

disgraceful scenes. . . eight or ten fights took place every day by two or three in the afternoon, the men stripping to the waist.

A correspondent described how:

a posse of prostitutes of the very lowest class were collected about this spot, to solicit, and afterwards, in many cases, rob their victims, the sailors. . . loafers, crimps and idle vagabonds of every description were loitering about, impeding the public thoroughfare.

And even at the time when the first respectable middle-class shoppers were coming over from Gosport on the new ferries, the area was still known as 'The Devil's Acre' – 'of twenty-one structures, fifteen are pubs.'

Whatever the conditions near the landing points on either side of the Harbour, passengers could be sure that they would be encouraged (sometimes in no uncertain terms!) to choose between the rival firms' boats. There was a good deal of bumping and boring among the boats of the opposing companies as the representatives from each firm touted for custom on the pontoons. The fierce competition between the companies brought the fare down to $^1/_2$d. An angry letter to the *Portsmouth Evening News* on 8 January 1892, contains evidence of some of the unpleasantness travellers had to contend with:

> Sir, isn't it time something was done to protect ladies crossing the water in the Portsea launches from being compelled to listen to filthy language used not only by passengers but often by the company's employees as well? Only today, a lady friend of mine had occasion to cross to Portsea and had to sit in the launch while two men were fighting and using the most disgusting language. Hoping something will be done to improve the existing state of affairs on the ferry and thanking you in anticipation.
> Disgusted, Gosport.

But while the more sedate complained about the unseemliness of it all, the youngsters thought it great fun. The rival launches sometimes made the crossing very close together, and Gosport boys on their way to Portsmouth schools looked forward to a daily contest as to who could change boats the most times in one crossing. Indeed, it was 'de rigueur' among them that each should finally disembark at Portsea on a different boat from that one on which he had started!

But, to everyone's relief, except the boys, the two companies reached a compromise before a major disaster could intervene. In 1888, it was agreed that a launch of each company would leave each side of the Harbour at the same time, signalled by the ringing of a loud bell, whereupon the next set of passengers would be issued with a ticket for the other company, and so on throughout the day. Eventually, all the ferry takings were pooled and shared out equally between the 'Old' and 'New' companies, as they soon became known in preference to those enormous official titles although the floating bridge company, with its different route

Beatrix Potter at the age of eighteen. The famous children's authoress recorded her impressions of a visit to the Harbour in 1884.

across the Harbour, maintained a lofty independence.

The skippers of the ferry boats have always had a deserved reputation for skill, unflappability and the ability to get on with their vital job, come what may in the shape of bad weather or other troubles. More than one of them has, over the years, performed acts of bravery in the line of duty. For example, on Easter Monday 1885, on a pitch-black night with the wind blowing a gale, a marine on one of the 'New' company's launches tried to commit suicide by jumping in to the toiling waters in mid-Harbour. The captain, William Cottrell, at once handed the wheel over to the mate and plunged in. He reached the man and managed to swim ashore with him at Gosport. Another time, this same brave sailor rescued a little boy who had begun to drown while swimming with his brother near Point. Later, the grateful mother of this little boy sent a letter and a silver pencil to Cottrell, who treasured these mementoes for the rest of his life. Indeed, many people, particularly children playing in the water off the steps at the Sally Port, owed their lives to rescues by watermen and ferrymen such as Cottrell, his cousin Albert, Charlie Pound and Dick Crafts. As a reporter for *Pink's Pictorial* was told when he visited the Point watermen, 'there's lots around here has saved dozens, but they don't make no talk about it.'

Considering such tales of bravery, it is particularly sad that those watermen who couldn't or wouldn't join the new companies or afford a steam launch of their own were beginning to suffer real hardship as a result of the new regular services. Yet proudly they stayed on, at Gosport, Portsmouth Hard and Point, with their cries of 'A trip to the *Victory*, gentlemen!' Many of them entered their wherries in the popular Point Regattas at the turn of the century. The race course was from Point, around the *Victory*, and back across the Harbour to the finishing post, marked by the splendid new Isle of Wight paddle steamer, *Duchess of Kent*. Famous wherries included *Why Not*, *The Pride of Portsea*, *There She Goes*, and *Flying Cloud*; manned by watermen Dukes, Grist, Batchelor, White and Cottrell. These Regattas were a tremendously popular Harbour attraction, with amusing events such as greasy pole and pillow fight competitions, 'tub races' and 'coal shovellers' races (when four-man crews used coal shovels instead of oars) as well as the rowing races.

As seaside holidays to Portsmouth and Southsea became ever more fashionable, to be rowed out to the *Victory* by a boatman was an absolute must. Beatrix Potter, the children's author, left an account of such a visit with her parents in 1884:

> At the Pier-end was a broad, yellow-whiskered man who. . . had brought round a large old boat resembling a tub, into which we were put as prisoners, not without difficulty owing to the swell from two or three steamers and tugs which positively seem to swarm here. . . when once we were firmly captured the naval gentleman suddenly relented and became very communicative, and took us for a very pleasant row to the *Victory*.

The last years of Queen Victoria's century were flourishing times for our area. The Dockyard and shore establishments were busy. Great progress was made in the field of public amenities in a very short time. In 1891, Gosport's first park was laid out on the former gypsy encampment of Ewer Common, and in the same year the first public library was opened in the town. A railway was laid to the new resort of Lee-on-the-Solent. The old Dolphin tavern became a fire-station. Portsmouth citizens saw the building of several

Two ladies walk along a landing stage at Gosport while a boatman sorts out his oars.

An Edwardian view of the Harbour from the base of Fort Blockhouse, with H.M.S. St Vincent *in the foreground and* Camper & Nicholson's *in the background.*

A steam launch at one of the Gosport landing stages, c. 1900.

A small ferry boat docks at Old Portsmouth. One of the advertisements on view offers 30 de Reszke cigarettes for one shilling.

A striking drawing of the Dockyard fire of December 1913, when two lives were lost and the Semaphore Tower was destroyed; the latter was rebuilt later in the same style.

The Hard, c. 1904. Prominent buildings include the Portsea Post Office and the 'Ship Anson'.

Portsmouth City Museums

schools, the telephone exchange, the public baths, the central library and the Roman Catholic Cathedral. The appearance of the impressive bell-tower, built for Holy Trinity Church in 1889, and the imposing new Guildhall which was completed a year later added impressive landmarks on each side of the Harbour. The 1893 Guide Book to Southsea enthused about the improvements, and added that the area boasted 'the finest Harbour in the world, possessing every advantage without one single disadvantage.'

But behind this glittering facade, the three ferry companies were not without their troubles. The small passenger launches were often badly over-crowded and had no protection from bad weather. Landing and embarking were hazardous tasks, particularly for ladies encumbered by the long dresses of the period who had to hop down off the boats in an undignified manner. A story is told of an artilleryman who strode boldly onto a launch from Portsea landing stage after a convivial evening. Unable to check his step, he walked straight over the side of the boat and into the water! Luckily, he was hooked aboard with the aid of the curved end of a walking-stick. Meanwhile, the floating bridge company's takings had been

reduced, thanks to the increased competition from the other two ferry undertakings, and it suffered a double misfortune in the 1890s. First, the *Albert* bridge sank at its moorings in 1891 and had to be sold for scrap, fetching a dismal sum of £360, and was eventually replaced at a cost of £7950 by the *Duchess of York* which was advertised as 'being lit by electricity throughout'. But the second setback was more costly still. During a fierce gale in 1893, the other bridge, *Alexandra*, together with one of the company's passenger launches, took such a battering from the wind and waves that they, too, sank at their moorings. The huge bridge was sub-merged in such a way as to disrupt the normal passage of the new *Duchess of York*; becoming entangled with the chains. Matters were made worse when a Dockyard gang, halfway through the task of attempting to salvage and repair the bridge, were called away to another job. The bridge was left suspended in slings, and when the rescue work was resumed later it was found that the hawsers had cut right through the hull. So the floating bridge service ceased to exist for nearly three months, to the annoyance of its many users, including by now the delivery horse-and-traps from the larger Portsmouth shops to the Gosport side.

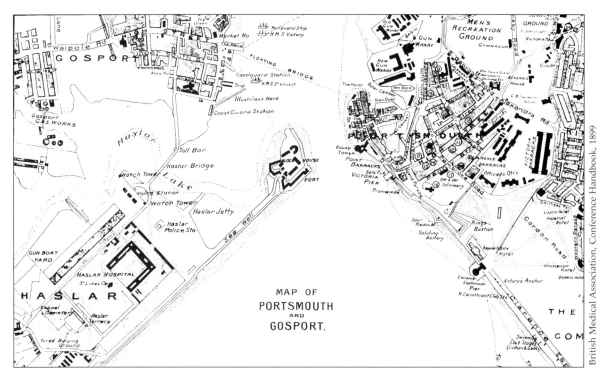

British Medical Association, Conference Handbook, 1899

1880s' map of the Harbour area illustrating a vastly different sea front at Gosport compared to that of today. Note the positions of the anchored ships in the Harbour and also the 'Turks Burying Ground' at Haslar – was it this that gave Gosport its earlier nickname of 'Turk Town'?

Gosport Museum Collection

A poor quality picture, but included because it is a rare view of the forerunner of today's Hard Interchange, together with what is described as the 'new' Harbour railway station. This belated addition to the Portsmouth railway scene provided a tremendous improvement for Victorian travellers, c. 1885.

Record of the first meeting of the 'Port of Portsmouth Steam Launch and Towing Company', a forerunner of today's Gosport Ferry company.

Floating Bridge and Steam Launches.

Portsmouth and Gosport Floating Bridge, leaves Point, Broad Street, for Gosport, as follows:—Bridge every half-hour, from 7.30 a.m. till 9 p.m.; Sundays 1-15 to 10 p.m. Launches every ten minutes, from 7-15 a.m. till 11 p.m.

Portsea and Gosport Steam Launches leave the Hard, Portsea, for Gosport every six minutes from 6 a.m. till 11-30 p.m. Sundays, 9 a.m. till 10-30 p.m.

Boat Fares

	s.	d.
To *Victory*, from Point or Hard, by wherry, single journey, 6d.; by time, 2s. per hour, for small parties.		
To Fareham, for one passenger and not exceeding four	3	6
For more than four and not exceeding eight ..	4	6
To all Ships lying in Portchester Lake or Fountain Lake	1	6
To Portchester, for one passenger & not exceeding four	2	6
For more than four and not exceeding eight ..	3	6

These Fares do not include waiting and returning with passengers

Excursions by Water.

PORTSMOUTH HARBOUR.—The *Blanche* runs up and down to view H. M. Ships, etc., daily, leaving Clarence Pier about 10 a.m. and about every hour after during the day; calling at Victoria Pier 5 minutes later. Fare 6d.

RYDE.—Cheap Return Tickets are issued on Week Days from Portsmouth Harbour and Southsea Pier by 11-20 a.m. and subsequent Boats; on Sundays by 12-15 noon and subsequent Boats. On Week Days from Ryde Pier Gates to Portsmouth Harbour and Southsea Pier by 11-15 a.m. and subsequent Boats up to 6-15 p.m. inclusive; on Sundays by 11 a.m. and subsequent Boats up to 5-5 p.m. inclusive. Fares (including Pier Tolls)—First Class and Saloon 1/4; Third Class 1/-,

N.B. On the return journey, visitors are warned to make enquiries before embarking, as tickets issued by one Company are not recognised by another.

ISLE OF WIGHT—Cheap Return Tickets will be issued Sandown, Shanklin, Ventnor, Newport, Cowes, and other tions on the Isle of Wight and Isle of Wight Central Rail-, on Week Days from Portsmouth Harbour Station and

An advertisement from 1899 for various ferry and sight-seeing trips in and around the Harbour.

Portsmouth Harbour Ferry Co. Ltd

British Medical Association, Conference Handbook, 1899

The unwelcome and unexpected disruption led to suggestions at a Portsmouth Council meeting early in 1894 for improving communications between the two towns. The floating bridge came in for much criticism: 'There being only one bridge ready on the chains, serious delay is caused to traffic until damage is put right; and when it happens in mid-harbour, horses and vans are exposed to the weather for hours; and if both chains break, and the bridge drifts out to sea, the consequences would be serious,' said one councillor. More pertinent points were made. The number of journeys per day was said to be inadequate. The approaches to the bridge on both sides of the Harbour were in a wretched condition. Floating pontoons, to be placed in trenches, were suggested as the answer to the steep gradient which handicapped the horse traffic when embarking on or leaving the bridge at high tide. Sir William Pink went so far as to draw

up plans for a completely new vehicular ferry to replace the floating bridge. He envisaged the use of paddlewheel ferry boats for vehicles and passengers, which would maintain a fifteen-minute service and would be manned by the crews of the present launches and floating bridges. (Oddly enough, the design of the proposed new boats bore an uncanny resemblance to our present-day Harbour ferries.)

But the floating bridge company sailed through these strong tides of criticism. Soon the regular service was running smoothly again, and later in 1894, the company appointed Mr Harry Sinclair as manager. During the twenty years that he occupied this office, Mr Sinclair, who was a former Master-at-Arms aboard the Royal Yacht, became a popular local character and presided over a prosperous period in the company's fortunes. Very conscious of the vital role of the floating

The Secretary of the Admiralty presents his

compliments to Mr R.E. Froude

and begs to enclose two *Ticket s for the*

"Jumna" *to witness the review at Spithead*

on 23rd July, 1887, and regrets that the limited

number for whom accommodation can be provided

prevents his sending more.

Robert Froude's invitation to the Spithead Review of 1887 which celebrated Queen Victoria's Golden Jubilee. R.E. Froude was the first operational manager of the Admiralty Experiment Works (now D.E.R.A.).

Admiralty.

An artist's impression of the Diamond Jubilee Review of 1897. The impressive display of Britain's naval strength consisted of 165 ships moored in five lines. Large crowds watched as the Royal Yacht Victoria and Albert *with the Prince of Wales on board steamed up and down the lines of ships.*

bridge, he made various improvements and also introduced three new launches, *Phoenix*, *Viva* and *Sandringham*, each of which remained in service for many years.

All the ferry companies flourished during the occasion of the Queen's Diamond Jubilee Review of the fleet, when the Harbour was full of the mighty ships of the new Navy. Thousands watched this biggest display ever of Britain's sea power. Even the magnificent sight of the massed vessels was eclipsed by the appearance of the first turbine-propelled ship, C.J. Parsons' *Turbinia*, which thrilled the crowds by roaring round the Harbour at speeds of over thirty knots. But the next time large gatherings of people thronged the Harbour the occasion was a sad one. On 1 February 1901, Queen Victoria's body was borne across the Solent from Osborne. William Gates described the scene:

> As the Royal Yacht entered the Harbour the last gleams of the winter sun shone forth; the

sky, for a few moments, glowed red, and then grey mist veiled the ships.

Early in the new century, the Gosport and Alverstoke Urban District Council, which had been the governing body since 1894, began to discuss the possible take-over by themselves of the ferry companies – but the scheme faded into the background as public attention became focused instead on the vexed issue as to whether or not Gosport should become a Borough, a contentious subject which was not to be resolved until 1922. But, heeding the warning, the 'Old' and 'New' companies brought into service new, improved boats such as *Viceroy*, *King Edward*, *Venus*, *Ferry Queen* and *Vesta II*, while the floating bridge company introduced another launch, *Sir John Baker*. All of these boats were to give stout service until long after the First World War. Meanwhile, the floating bridge company rebuilt and enlarged the Portsmouth landing stage and improved the slipway at Gosport.

The Royal Yacht Osborne, *a handsome paddle streamer, was a familiar sight in the Harbour in the years before the First World War.*

Charles Stapleton, Superintendent of the Floating Bridge Company between 1897 and 1925.

A view of the Gunwharf gate c.1905, with guard and a young looker-on.

Gosport Museum Collection

A busy scene at Gosport Hard almost a hundred years ago. Passengers await the ferry boats and floating bridge, while H.M.S. St Vincent is moored close to Fort Blockhouse.

R.N. Submarine Museum, Gosport

Old and new in this photograph of 1907. Seven men balance carefully on the latest sea-going vessel, a submarine, while the venerable H.M.S. Victory looks on placidly.

Gosport Museum Collection

The landing stages of the ferry boat companies were quite exposed and subject to tides, as may be seen from this photograph of a century ago.

Portsmouth City Museums

The Hard, Portsea, c. 1905. In the foreground is the railway line from the Harbour station extending to the South Railway Jetty in the Dockyard.

Gosport Society Collection

A painting by Gosport's most famous artist, Martin Snape, shows one of Gosport's landing stages with the Camper & Nicholson and Ratsey & Lapthorn buildings prominent.

Portsmouth City Council

The sight of livestock crossing the Harbour in an open boat would cause a stir today, but in 1909 it was commonplace. In this photograph, boys have suspended their fishing activities to watch cattle being carefully loaded on board.

In the early years of the twentieth century, European nations vied to build bigger and better warships. One of the most famous was H.M.S. Dreadnought, built at Portsmouth. In this picture, King Edward VII can be seen at the launching ceremony, towards the front of the flag-bedecked stand, while the huge iron walls of the ship dwarf the people below. For the record, H.M.S. Dreadnought, in model form, was tested in the ship tank at Haslar.

Private Collection

Portsmouth City Museums

It is 1906 and H.M.S. Dreadnought has just been launched. The silhouettes of the vessels in the Harbour together with threatening skies and cold waves seem to paint a sombre foreboding of conflict to come.

The stern of H.M.S. Dreadnought *towers above the busy scene in the Harbour.*

The ferries prospered. The terminals teemed with travellers – among them children who today recall memories of those long-ago times. All of them remember the crammed decks and the difficulties of getting on or off in rough weather. Two ladies recall playing on the muddy beach at Gosport and the untidy litter of wooden blocks and slippery seaweed; people were frequently falling over like ninepins, one gentleman remembers. One of the little kiosks on the Gosport side housed an old lady who served many a little child with a halfpenny mixed bag of dusty allsorts. For some youngsters, a trip on the clanking, rattling floating bridge was a special treat; for businessmen and shopkeepers, it was a transport facility that enabled them to deliver their wages across the Harbour. For one dog, the floating bridge journey meant a morning's ratting in the Camper and Nicholson's yard. This animal, in fact, became a familiar sight on the bridge. He

was owned by the manager of Snook & Sons' grocery shop in Portsmouth High Street – where he also acted as a ratter – but often, hearing the arrival of the bridge at Broad Street, he would rush to the landing stage and take the trip across to Gosport by himself!

Great excitement came to the area in 1905 with the combined review of the British and French fleets in the presence of Edward VII. Gosport and Portsea houses and inns were gaily decorated with flags and bunting while the floating bridge zcrossed the Harbour festooned in red, white and blue. A house on Gosport Beach was covered with signal flags, although a section of them had been so arranged as to read, unfortunately, 'Fever On Board – Send A Doctor'. The following year saw another visit by the King, who christened the famous ironclad H.M.S. *Dreadnought* in front of crowds of well-wishers.

Portsmouth City Museums

The 1905 boom defence under test. This comprised a large number of timber baulks secured by steel hawsers; each one was over 30 feet long and armed with steel spikes.

Portsmouth City Museums

Passengers take their ease on the Isle of Wight ferry Alexandra *while a launch from Gosport approaches the landing stage under the watchful gaze of grey warships. A coaling hulk can be seen anchored in mid-Harbour.*

Victoria Pier, Sally Port. Built in 1842, the pier was the original embarkation point for Isle of Wight ferries. Note the attractive gazebo-style ticket office to the right.

A charming study of Gosport Hard c.1910, showing the ticket offices of both ferry companies. Note the elegant lamps and also the loungers by the Gambier drinking fountain – the latter, incidentally, stands at present almost on the same spot, having been moved to other locations in previous years!

Portsmouth City Museums

The Iron Duke, *a battleship of 25,000 tons, was launched in the Harbour in October 1912. In this picture, the ship is moored up harbour while men scoop up the grease used during the launch from the slipway.*

Portsmouth City Museums

Southsea sea front – Clarence Esplanade c. 1910. The recreational aspects of the Harbour have always played a large part in local life.

Portsmouth City Museums

Passengers including a smartly-dressed gentleman lounging against the rail and a smiling young lady with a parcel pose with the crew for this photograph of one of the smart new steam launches of the 1890s. The masts and rigging of other vessels in the Harbour provide a picturesque backdrop.

Portsmouth City Museums

An attractive view of the Harbour in 1881. Ratsey & Lapthorn's sailmakers and Camper & Nicholson's boatbuilders establishments can be seen to the right, while Beach Street stretches away to the left. The familiar landmark of Holy Trinity bell-tower is absent – it was not added until 1887.

Early submarines in Haslar Creek.

The submarine Holland I *in Portsmouth Harbour c. 1904.*

A tranquil scene from days long ago. Gosport beach was a fascinating place for children to play or for their elders to watch the ships go by.

Tower House, Old Portsmouth.

Portsmouth City Council

'When Britain really ruled the waves…' An artist's impression of the complete Royal Navy in the early part of the reign of George V 'our sailor king'.

In 1918, the seascape was very different, but today people crossing the Harbour still disembark at the same spot in Portsmouth. Note that every man is wearing both hat and tie! H.M.S. Victory, *seen in the background, was to be removed into dry dock a few years later.*

Gosport Society Collection

UNDER
TWO FLAGS.

THE

Official Programme

OF THE

VISIT OF THE FRENCH FLEET TO PORTSMOUTH,

7th, 8th, 9th, 10th, 11th, 12th, 13th & 14th AUGUST, 1905.

6D.

Printed and Published by :—

GALE & POLDEN, Ltd.,

NELSON WORKS, EDINBURGH ROAD, PORTSMOUTH,

LONDON AND ALDERSHOT.

Gale and Polden

Programme cover of the eight-day visit of the French Fleet to Portsmouth in 1905. This was a huge publicity event designed to help cement the growing friendship between the two nations – the 'entente cordiale' – after years of hostility.

THE DAILY ROUTINE OF A MAN OF WAR.

BOATSWAIN'S MATES' PIPE.

TIME. A.M.	
5.35	"Hammock Stowers lash up and Stow Hammocks."
6.0	"All hands lash up and Stow Hammocks. Heave out! Heave out! Show a leg! Show a leg! Show a leg!"
6.15	"Hands to Cocoa."
6.35	"Out Pipes: Clean out Spit Kids."
6.40	"Clean lower deck: Hands fall in on the upper deck."
7.50	"Cooks to the Galley: Place Spit Kids."
8.0	"Breakfast "Hands to clean in white working dress."
8.45	"Out pipes: Clean up all decks for Divisions."
9.0	"Divisions for Inspection." Prayers are read after Inspection, and men are detailed for work.
11.45	"Cooks to the Galley."
12.0	Dinner.

Photo Gale & Polden]   6 inch Gun of H.M.S. Good Hope in Casemate.

P.M.	
12.30	"Hands muster for Grog." (The best time of the day).
1.10	"Out pipes: Clean out Spit Kids."
1.15	"Clean lower deck." Men are then detailed for work.
4.0	"Cooks to the Galley: Liberty men fall in: Hands shift into Night Clothing."
5.0	"Hands to Fire Quarters."
7.20	"Cooks to the Galley," and at 7.30 "Supper."
7.50	"Clear up all decks," and at 8.0 "Stand by Hammocks."
9.0	Rounds.
9.55	"Out Pipes."
10.0	Piped down.

Gale and Polden

'The Daily Routine of a Man of War'. A fascinating description of the ordinary sailor's daily life in 1905.

Tourist souvenirs are nothing new. In 1905, visitors to the Harbour could take home either of these novelty souvenir spoons for seven shillings and sixpence; quite a lot to pay, so presumably the spoons were well made.

Transport facilities in 1914 had reached heights undreamed of a century earlier. The three ferry companies linked their regular timetables not only to the railways at Harbour and Gosport stations but also to the new electric tram services that were spreading through the towns along the vastly improved roads. The fare was still only one halfpenny for foot passengers, although to take that exciting novelty, the motor car, across on the floating bridge cost $^1/_2$d for a return fare. Everything possible was done to keep the services going at all times; for example, one lady recalls that her father-in-law, Mr Bryant, who was chief engineer to the floating bridge company, was often called upon to work throughout the night with his men in order to maintain the service in good working order.

Electric lighting, still regarded by some with awe, illuminated the floating bridge landing stages now. But world events were soon to eclipse the bright Edwardian days. The 1914 fleet review had ended with a searchlight display when the ships manipulated their lights to set the Solent skies ablaze. Yet less than a month later, the lamps were going out all over Europe as the worst war known to the world began. As usual in this area, the war brought much activity as great provision was made to maintain the Navy – and as more and more men went to the front, women, for the first time, went to work in such places as Priddy's Hard. The 'Old' and 'New' companies' launches ran to and fro much as usual during the war. Military men were frequently transported to and fro by the ferries, and Mr Arthur Dorey, later to become a long-serving skipper on the service,

recalls an incident from these times when a group of skylarking soldiers didn't endear themselves to local travellers. These young men had amused themselves by throwing every one of the lifebuoys into the water during the crossing from Portsea. Mr Dorey remembers the captain, Mr Hoare, asking him to take over the wheel to bring the ferry in to the pontoon, while the latter went down to the deck to confront the roisterers. When the ferry landed, angry words and blows were exchanged, the police called – and the soldiers were ordered out in boats back into the Harbour to collect up every one of the floating lifebuoys!

The floating bridge company was more severely affected by the war than the rival ferries. Its passenger launches, *Sir John Baker*, *Sandringham* and *Viva* were requisitioned by the Admiralty for inspection duties at the Harbour entrance. Although the company received compensation money, it amounted to less than normal traffic receipts would have brought it. To make matters worse, several of the company's employees were called up for war work, with the result that the staff was mostly reduced to what the manager described as 'elderly men and boys and a few inefficients who have not been good enough for military service'.

But the bridges continued to run, and when the war ended, the launches that had been on Government duties were returned safely to their regular ferry duties. Normal services resumed in a world which was soon to be seen as a much changed place.

Chapter 7

THE GREAT 'ENDEAVOUR'

Like any other town, Gosport had its share of problems at the end of the war. Central government had made inadequate provision for the problems caused by the vast numbers of servicemen returning to peacetime Britain. With the nation's economy geared to wartime for so long, there were few jobs and some employers were able to exploit the position by keeping wages very low. There were also big cuts in government spending. By 1922, the *Evening News* was reporting 'a catalogue of reductions – big savings on Dockyard wages.'

Bad times seemed just around the corner – but out of the gloom came shafts of light in Gosport in the form of bright new civic achievements. The Chairman of Gosport Urban District Council just after the war was Mr W.C. Harvey. He had long believed that the sea approach to the town should be tidied up and made both attractive and useful. His scheme were adopted by the council. At a cost of £59,983, an esplanade was to be constructed, gardens laid and a new quay and pontoon for the ferry services was to be built. The work was undertaken by J. Price and Co., and the project was begun in 1922. It was a complicated task. About three acres of land had to be reclaimed, and a channel was dredged through the Coldharbour mud. The work involved another alteration to a familiar landmark in the town; the ramparts next to the Conservative Club at the far end of High Street were taken down and used as in-filling at the shore.

By the end of the year, the main promenade of the new gardens was finished and the 40-ton pontoon had been carefully placed in position with very little disruption to the normal running of the ferries.

The main pathway was named 'Harvey's Promenade' in honour of the originator of the scheme. It was a splendid start for the newly-formed Borough of Gosport, which also carried on the good work of improving the town through the construction of the esplanade at Stokes Bay and the provision of a general face-lift of all the town's open spaces, whilst developing new council housing at Forton. When the new Ferry Gardens were formally opened in 1925, the contrast between old and new must have been tremendous. In place of the untidy muddle of stone piers and the irregular grass and mud shoreline, there now appeared trim gardens with neat rows of newly-planted trees, radial paths and flower-beds, the centre one containing Admiral Gambier's impressive old drinking fountain, which had previously stood outside the Market House.

While Gosport's seafront was being revolutionized, an important change took place also in the Harbour itself. In 1922, that venerable vessel H.M.S. *Victory* was removed from her moorings on the Gosport side into Dry Dock No. 2 in the Dockyard to undergo extensive repairs and restoration. This was a serious blow to the remaining watermen, who had gained a vital income for many years from rowing visitors to view *Victory's* wooden walls at sixpence a time. Certainly there was concern in Gosport at the imminent disappearance of one of the town's tourist attractions. The Mayor-elect, Jesse Lee, in a deputation with Mr Harvey and Mr Pilcher, urged the Portsmouth Commander-in-Chief to put *Victory* back into the water when she was restored. But her seriously decaying state finally decided the argument – and *Victory* became a tourists' delight, but, sadly for Gosport, on the other side of the Harbour.

Forgotten times at Gosport waterfront – H.M.S. Victory *rides at anchor near Clarence Square.*

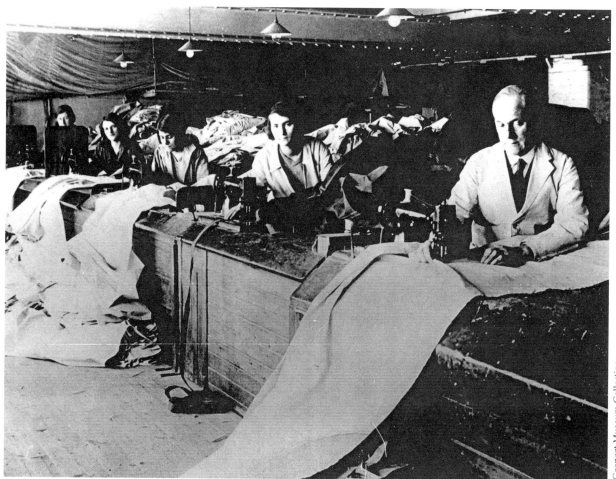

Girls at Ratsey & Lapthorn making spinnaker sails, c. 1929. From left: Phyllis Colbourn, Ida Sands, Gladys McGuirk, Sylvia Miskin, with their foreman George Leaf.

Until the 1920s, H.M.S. Victory *was anchored afloat near Gosport foreshore. This striking study of the famous ship dates from the late nineteenth century.*

A wealth of period detail may be seen in this 1930s' study of Ferry Gardens.

95

Southsea Beach in the early 1920s.

GOSPORT PONTOON
AND
SOUTH PARADE PIER STEAMERS.
DAILY EXCURSIONS
BY
S.S. "PRINCESSA,"
S.S. "SANDRINGHAM" AND "SIR JOHN BAKER,"
TO
SEAVIEW, ISLE OF WIGHT.

GOSPORT PONTOON, DEP.	9.30	2.30		
S. PARADE PIER, DEP.	10.0	11.20	3.0	4.30	6.30
SEAVIEW PIER, ARR.	10.30	11.50	3.30	5.0	7.0
SEAVIEW PIER, DEP.	10.35	12.0	3.45	6.0	7.0
S. PARADE PIER, ARR.	11.5	12.30	4.15	6.30	7.30
GOSPORT PONTOON, ARR.		1.0			8.0

FARES include all Pier Tolls.
SINGLE 1/6 Children under 12, half-price. RETURN 2/6.
COWES. COWES. COWES. COWES.
REGATTA WEEK.
CHEAP EVENING EXCURSIONS
BY
S.S. PRINCESSA or S.S. SANDRINGHAM,
commencing
SUNDAY, 30th JULY, 1922,
AND
EVERY EVENING DURING THE WEEK
(EXCEPT FIREWORK NIGHT).
Leave Gosport Pontoon 6.0 p.m.
„ Portsea Pontoon 6.10 p.m.
„ South Parade Pier 6.30 p.m.
Returning to Portsea Pontoon and Gosport Pontoon 10.15 p.m.
FARE RETURN 1s. 6d.
BOOK EARLY GOSPORT
FLOATING BRIDGE OFFICE.

Pleasure trips to Seaview and Cowes in Regatta Week are on offer from Gosport and Southsea in this advertisement from 1922.

CLARENCE PIER.
PAVILION HEATED.
MATINEES WED. & SAT., at 3.0.
NIGHTLY at 7.30.
ARCHIE WALLEN
AND
FARCE.
9 ARTISTES 9
UNANIMOUS OPINION:
" Better than ever."
LAST WEEK of " FARCE."

EXTRA ATTRACTIONS.
NIGHTLY CHANGE OF PROGRAMME.
THURSDAY, at 7.30,
BEAUTY AND FANCY DRESS
COMPETITION
FOR LADIES AND GENTLEMEN,
BIG PRIZES.
1st Prize (Beauty), £1 1s.; Second, 10s. 6d.; Third, 5s. 1st Prize (Fancy Dress), £1 1s.; Second, 10s. 6d.; Third, 5s. Audience will judge. Entry Forms at Pier.
FRIDAY, SPECIAL REQUEST NIGHT.
SATURDAY (MATINEE), CHILDREN'S CHRISTMAS CARNIVAL, with Christmas Tree and Gigantic Santa Claus Stocking. Archie Wallen's Performing Donkey. Toys and Balloons given away
Ring up 2103. Book Your Seats Early.
Pier Toll 2d. Pavilion 3d. (inc. Tax).
Reserved Seats 6d. extra (inc. Tax).

SATURDAY, 7.30.
FAREWELL & GALA NIGHT.
ADMISSION THIS EVENING ONLY.
Pier Toll 2d., Pavilion 8d. (including Tax).
Reserved Seats 7d. extra (including Tax).

Clarence Pier playbill c. 1922.

Old Portsmouth, with, to the left, the Tower House, former home of the distinguished marine artist William Wyllie, and the Round Tower to the right.

Meanwhile it was back to business for the three companies. Each had added new launches to their fleets – the *Varos*, *Ferry King*, *Ferry Belle* and *Princessa*. The last three of these boats had been built by Camper and Nicholson since 1918 and were all slightly updated versions of the style of launch whose pattern had been laid down by the *Queen* in 1884 and which was to continue to be successful for another four decades.

The bustle of activity at the smart new Ferry Gardens produced an air of prosperity at the entrance to Gosport, enhanced by the developing shopping centre in High Street where shops were filled with an increasing variety of goods. But although Gosport's population grew considerably in the inter-war years, and the new housing estates in Brockhurst and Elson expanded the town's area, the economic climate was hardly conducive to further improvements. Dockyard pay was low, other employment sporadic and life became hard. Successive economy drives began to run down the Royal Navy. Having made such a promising start, the new Borough was forced to

cut costs in all directions and behind the smiling seafront, many of the older houses were falling into decay while the once-picturesque alleys and courts aged into decrepitude because there was no money to do anything about them.

Neither were the ferry companies without their troubles. When the 'New' company announced a fare increase from ¹/₂d to 1d in 1922, there was an outcry. Gosport Labour Party held a protest meeting, and plans were afoot to boycott the service until the company agreed to retain the halfpenny fare for the rush-hour boats. (Amazingly to think of in these days of taken-for-granted inflation, the fares remained unchanged throughout the 1920s and 1930s!) A few years later, in 1927, the new pontoon on the Gosport side began to sink during a storm. For a little while, travellers managed to board the swaying vessels from the damaged pontoon, but soon one end sank beneath the water and disruption and delays occurred while the boats were landed elsewhere. Apparently, the pontoon was not fully operational again until 1930.

Gosport Hard and the floating bridge landing stage in the 1920s.

The American steam yacht Crusader, *which was sunk by enemy bombers in the Harbour during the Second World War.*

But the old floating bridge service suffered the most in the inter-war period. The decline of the company began, as we have seen, during the First World War, and now running costs began to mount alarmingly. In 1918, the company had 21 employees whose wages ranged between 7/6 and £3.4.5$^{1}/_{2}$d a week, making a wages bill of £29.4.7d – a trivial total to us, perhaps, but it represented a 30% increase since 1867, during which time daily receipts had remained almost static. A new toll house and landing stage at Portsmouth incurred extra costs. By 1923, the Directors' Report conceded a massive decrease of £1968 in takings from the previous year. The company tried hard to improve matters – the car fare was reduced from 1/3 to 1/-, and regular round-the-harbour pleasure trips were commenced – but financially, there was little improvement. In 1924, the company was approached by Portsmouth Corporation with a view to buying the service, but sadly for everyone in hindsight, nothing came of these negotiations.

There was, of course, still a considerable delivery trade on the floating bridge. Many firms and drivers preferred to use the bridge rather than take the wearisome drive via Fareham – but several of them recall difficulties in getting on or off. Mr Robbins, who used to drive the 'Maypole' van over from Portsmouth to Gosport, remembers the steep climb off the bridge if the tide was low. And there were sometimes dramatic accidents. More than once, George Street, one-time captain on the floating bridge, was called upon to rescue dray horses that had slipped on the icy ramps in the winter and fallen into the sea, still attached to their wagons. As the horses struggled, George plunged into the freezing waters to rescue them from drowning by cutting their ropes, a brave deed which gained him medals from the Royal Humane Society.

The floating bridge had a boost when, in 1930, the Dockyard decided to use its services for conveying coal to government establishments in Gosport. This increase of traffic swelled weekly takings by eight or nine pounds. Despite this and increased car ownership, the depression of trade in the 1930s together with a series of very poor summers led to more financial troubles for the company. Indeed, in 1939, the floating bridge's average daily takings amounted to less than £12 – a disappointing figure when it is considered that the average was £9.6.4d per day nearly a century before.

But as always, special events brought profits to all the ferry companies. The fleet review of 1937, 'Pompey's' growing popularity on Saturday afternoons on the terraces and the King and Queen's departure for Canada from Portsmouth in 1939, all drew crowds. Syd Stephens, one of the pre-war ferry skippers, recalled that at the latter event

All attention in this photograph from the late 1930s is focused on H.M.S. Hood *leaving the Harbour. The water tower of H.M.S.* Vernon *and the old power station buildings are also prominent.*

Gosport Society Collection

The News, Portsmouth

One of the new post-war ferry boats, the Varos, *unloads passengers on a winter's day. The men are about to try to disentangle their bicycles from the piled heap in the bows!*

there were so many people on the Portsea pontoon that it nearly sank under the strain, and six ferry boats had to be brought up to take people off safely. Meanwhile, Portsmouth people used the ferries to visit Gosport 'for a breath of fresh air' – there was more open countryside hereabouts in those days, and hikes to Lee, blackberrying at Browndown and a swim at the fine open-air pool were popular attractions.

During this inter-war period, a number of very elegant yachts were built at Camper and Nicholson with sails provided by Ratsey and Lapthorn. These fine creations for the affluent yachting set provided not only considerable employment but also eagerly-awaited spectacles for local people. The most exciting occasion was undoubtedly the launching in April 1934 of Sir Thomas Sopwith's yacht *Endeavour*. Everyone was agog to see this new Universal 'J' Class yacht, which was to be the British challenger for the America's Cup, and which was also acclaimed as Charles Nicholson's design masterpiece. Every available ferry-boat was packed to capacity, peo-

ple crowded the shores and Camper and Nicholson's had to adopt a ticket system in their yard, so vast was the number of enthusiasts who wanted to witness the launching at close quarters. The huge yacht, which was to come so close to winning the Cup, slid into the water to the accompaniment of huge cheers against a gay background of flags and bunting. It was in every sense a local occasion, for the celebration luncheon on launching day was held at Meotti's little Swiss Restaurant in the High Street. Later in the year, people crowded into Ferry Gardens where the results of the individual races for the America's Cup were flashed onto an illuminated scoreboard. There was tremendous enthusiasm for this product of the town – and indeed for Sopwith's next yacht, *Endeavour II*, the biggest cutter ever built in Britain, which was launched in 1936. It is perhaps typical of the country at this time that although very many local people were truly badly-off, living in a totally different world to those who could afford to race yachts, the warmth and enthusiasm for 'special occasions' transcended their personal troubles.

The launching from Camper & Nicholson's yard of the Endeavour, *the British challenger for the America's Cup, in April 1934, caused great local excitement. Hordes of visitors, including journalists and film-cameramen, crammed the Harbour shores to give the elegant yacht a fitting salutation.*

Private Collection

Indeed, it does appear to us in these more self-centred days that the 1930s was a period of sharing and caring, based on an attitude of self-responsibility, albeit that the divisions of social class were greater than they were today. The Portsmouth *Evening News* reported the many good deeds done for the poor by such societies as the 'Brotherhoods', and approvingly noted in December 1931 that it had been:

> a sober Christmas – the schoolmaster, working steadily in line with the social reformer, has decidedly succeeded in inculcating self-respect.

Feelings of local pride were strengthened by the introduction of 'Navy Week' in 1927. So many visitors flocked to see the fun that the idea was extended in subsequent years and the August Bank Holiday period saw the ferries carrying thousands of people across the Harbour to see the Navy at work and play. By the early thirties, as many as 150,000 attended Navy Week. A very discordant note was struck in 1932 when someone painted on the promenade at Southsea, 'National Government gives £10,000 for Navy Week and NOTHING for 3 million unemployed.' This graffiti was considered to be the work of 'supposed Communists' and the *Evening News* promised that there would be 'a

rough handling for the men responsible if they were found'.

Of course, there may have been some local ferry-users who wished that there was more money available for improving the levels of comfort on the boats. Many recall the somewhat spartan conditions. At busy times, the foredecks were crammed with passengers and bikes, the latter thrown in a heap and sometimes entangled together. Passengers less anxious to alight quickly could sit, if they could get through the crush in the days before the companies introduced barriers to guide people round the vessels in sensible order, on the raised upper deck amidships on the seats around the sides. According to more than one traveller, the below-deck cabins were best avoided. Some improvements in post-war design had somewhat alleviated the old 'bow-heavy' problem suffered by the earlier boats; but many a first-time traveller on a rough day must have eyed that unnerving collection of lifebuoys surrounding the outside of the aft rails with some alarm! Children probably regarded rough weather trips with much more equanimity. Mrs Bond remembers the excitement of a rough journey to Portsmouth when, as a girl, she was taken to the Theatre Royal to see a pantomime, recalling that it was tipping with rain and that everyone was battened down in the tiny cabin.

Private Collection

Endeavour makes her way into the Harbour from Camper & Nicholson's slipway. The sail-makers, Ratsey & Lapthorn, worked closely with the boat-builders on all their prestigious yachts.

Gosport Museum Collection

Between the wars, bows of yachts produced by Camper & Nicholson were laid up off Little Beach Street.

Gosport Museum Collection

Workmen from Camper & Nicholson oversee the erection of one of the enormous masts made for the 'J' Class yachts – 1934.

A view of Ratsey & Lapthorn from a painting by Martin Snape, c. 1928.

Gosport Museum Collection

But what the boats lacked in grace and comfort, they certainly made up for in sturdiness. Considering the fact that the little vessels were working daily with their stop-start journeys, and their heavy load of passengers, it is a splendid tribute to their original designers and builders that their long ferry life-span was then extended into pleasure and cruise services elsewhere. The skippers, too, were as tough and proud as their boats. They usually worked two spells a day for six days a week, the morning turn beginning before 5 a.m. when the boats were scrubbed down and coal and water loaded on. Winter days saw the skippers, dressed in oilskins and big boots, at the wheel behind the 'dodger' – a small wooden screen that served as their only protection from the icy wind and rain. Mr Hoare, a captain in the early 1930s, remembers working over sixty hours a week on the service. Another veteran skipper, Mr Arthur Dorey, recalls how they dealt with keeping the ferries running in fog before the days of radar. The first boat from Gosport had to give two long blasts on his whistle to let the Portsea-based boat know that he had started out. Then, by a system of whistle signals, the boats managed to find their careful way across to the other side, fin-

ishing with a couple of toots on the whistle to let the waiting launches on the opposite side know they'd arrived. Of course, there were delays – but never did the hundreds of dockers who used the early ferries fail to get to work.

Until 1931, one of the extra services provided by the floating bridge company was a launch to Priddy's Hard and the four training hulks for artificer apprentices which went under the collective name of 'Fisgard'. Old boys of Fisgard recall that this trip, from Flathouse on the Portsmouth side, took twenty minutes, and that it could be a pretty grim journey in bad weather. The older lads often ragged the younger ones on the trip – for example, any newcomers who happened to have come from Greenwich where they were still taught the hornpipe were required by their elder brethren to perform the dance on the ferry deck. Meanwhile, new ideas about linking Gosport and Portsmouth were being suggested. Some local people had the foresight to imagine the future development of travel, particularly with regard to the vast number of vehicles that would be used by an ever-increasing amount of the population. In 1931, the Mayor of Gosport, C.E. Davis, and

Councillor G.V. Northcott proposed the building of a new coastal road between Southampton and Portsmouth that would pass through Gosport and carry traffic under the Harbour by way of a tunnel. This exciting idea caused much local discussion. Quite apart from the obvious travel advantages – a tunnel could be used for twenty-four hours a day in all weather – correspondents to the local newspapers pointed out that Gosportonians would also be able to benefit from Portsmouth's better educational opportunites, have instant access to the comparatively cosmopolitan shopping centre, and take a share of the city's cheap electricity. But many shopkeepers foresaw the possibility of a complete collapse of trade in Gosport if ever such a convenient link between the two communities should come about. As Councillor C.E. Pilcher so eloquently commented:

> It would require archangels to know how to keep the people in Gosport when for a penny (the tunnel toll) they could all go to a large city. Give Gosport a chance before you go elsewhere!

Thus the arguments have continued over the years in similar vein.

All too soon, however, attention was to be focussed onto world, rather than local topics. War became a growing threat once more. The impact of the conflict has, of course, been well documented elsewhere with regard to this area, so we shall confine our comments to the particular effect the war had on the ferry services. As a town in the front line of danger, of necessity, Gosport was required to prepare early. On 6 July 1939, the whole town with the exception of the ferry pontoon was blacked out as a test for what was to come. This caused something of a problem to late arrivals from Portsmouth on the last night ferries, some of whom discovered that they did not know their way around Gosport's darkened streets as well as they thought they did! And it was not long before the Admiralty felt it necessary to requisition some of the ferry companies' boats for various war-time uses. The 'New' company had a brand-new boat called *Vadne* and that redoubtable skipper Arthur Dorey remembers vividly what happened to her.

Mr Dorey was told to take *Vadne* to Birdlime Point one Sunday morning and leave her there and return the next day. When he did return, he found about a hundred dockies aboard, all engaged in

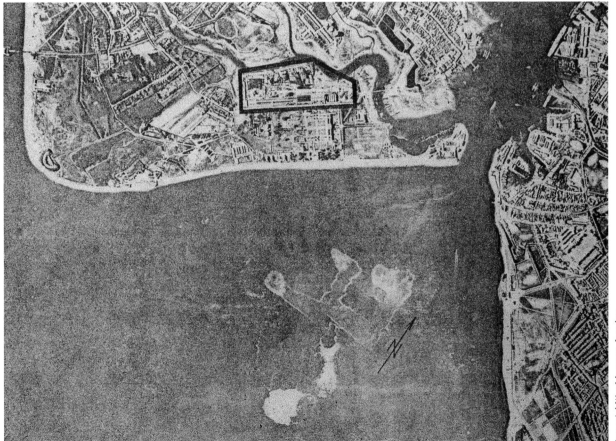

A photograph of the Harbour entrance taken by a German surveillance aeroplane during the war for use as guidance for bombers.

Imperial War Museum, London

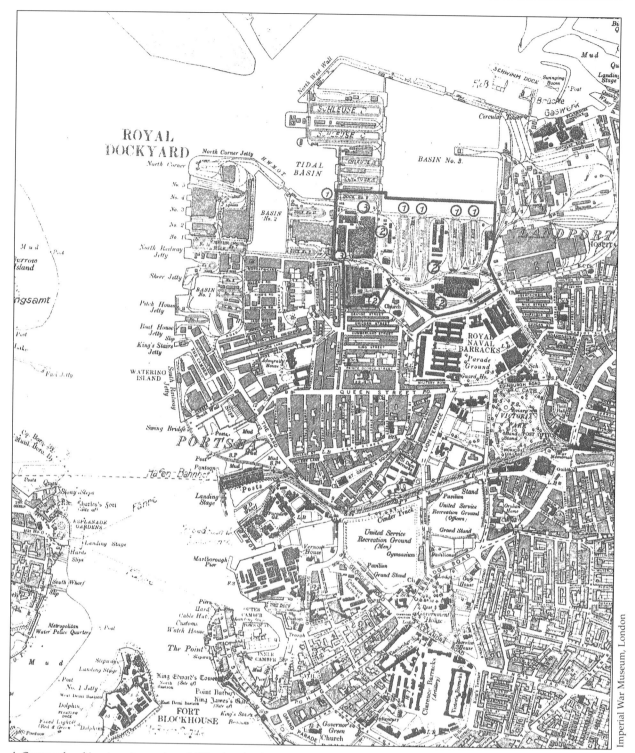

A German bombing target map from 1939, showing heavily-outlined key sites within the Dockyard. These maps were issued to Luftwaffe pilots and based on Ordnance Survey maps, overprinted in German.

Imperial War Museum, London

altering the boat almost out of all recognition. There was a new short mast, with three cross-trees and signal lights; the wheelhouse was being padded, the fenders had been ripped off. *Vadne* was being made ready for examination duties, and the following week, with Mr Dorey in charge, she steamed off to take up her watchdog duties. Later in the war, *Vadne* was shipped out to Freetown in West Africa to serve as a tender, and later as a landing stage, finally re-appearing in the Harbour after peace came to serve her original purpose as a ferryboat. Mr Dorey, meanwhile, went on to work on dredgers, preparing the channels which were to be of such value during 'Operation Overlord'.

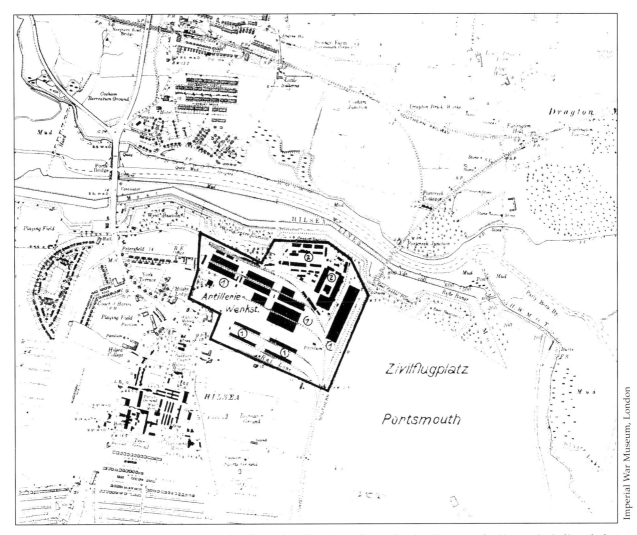

Wartime target bombing map for the Luftwaffe with Hilsea Barracks outlined. Portsmouth Airport is indicated, but not apparently as a target.

One of the two remaining floating bridges, the *Duchess of York*, was requisitioned by the transport department of the Ministry of War in May 1942 for a fee of £600. Normal ferry traffic was thrown into difficulties with the blackout – services ceased for a time after dark. During the heavy bombing, the floating bridge company's offices in Beach Street and its landing stage at Portsmouth were severely damaged. But the company at least took both pride and profit from its bridges being invaluable to the Admiralty and War Department as transporters of vehicles and explosives.

As the air raids began to batter away at Portsmouth and Gosport, naval pinnaces still had to cross the Harbour, blackout or not. A Voluntary Aid Detachment Nurse, Helen Long, arrived at the war-damaged Portsmouth Harbour railway station ready to take up duties at Haslar Hospital on the night of 11 November 1941, in the middle of a raid.

Mrs Long wrote this vivid account of that night:

> The air was heavy with the tantalising smell of seaweed, wet ropes, and tar, as with our cases we scuttled down to the water's edge, where we were to meet up with R.N.H. Haslar's pinnace. . . Tonight, with fires lighting the skies on both sides of the water, creating a gigantic fireworks display (for Gosport, too, was under attack), our skipper dropped anchor half-way across, and we sat (blacked-out, of course) and waited for the gunfire and bombing to die down.

During the same year, the Isle of Wight ferry *Portsdown* was blown up by a mine while on early morning duty. Mr Shilling, who worked for the Post Office for forty-one years, often taking the mail over to Gosport on the floating bridge, remembers that the huge mail cargo from the

More sites within the Harbour area, suggested as targets for the Luftwaffe.

Portsdown was rescued from the bottom of the sea and brought to the old welfare chapel in Stanhope Road where he and his colleagues laid the parcels and packets out to dry, stained and seaweed-bedecked as they were. Almost every item was sorted out and later delivered!

Later in the war, the massive 'Operation Overlord', with its immense building work and mass embarkations, was to provide great excitement. A project of a different kind, however, suggested and designed by an engineer by the name of E.W. Chalmers Kearney, never came to fruition. If it had, then crossing the Harbour both during and after the war would have been very different indeed. Kearney's scheme was to build a tunnel deep beneath the Harbour which would contain an electrically-driven railcar on a single rail, an idea which, he claimed, could take people across the Harbour in less than a minute. He approached the councils of both Portsmouth and Gosport with the scheme which he reckoned would cost about £400,000. Huge crowds attended meetings to hear the inventor explain his plans. As Mr Kearney said, 'The future development of our Borough (Gosport) depends on rapid and efficient communication.' At the outbreak of war, Kearney had suggested that such a tunnel could be adapted as a deep air-raid shelter, with people accommodated in tiered bunks within the tube. Public enthusiasm was considerable for his revolutionary idea, but alas, after the war, the councils voted against it on mainly financial grounds – although the tunnel principle was to re-appear in other forms in post-war proposals for crossing the Harbour.

Women workers employed at the Royal Naval Armament Dept, Priddy's Hard, during the Second World War.

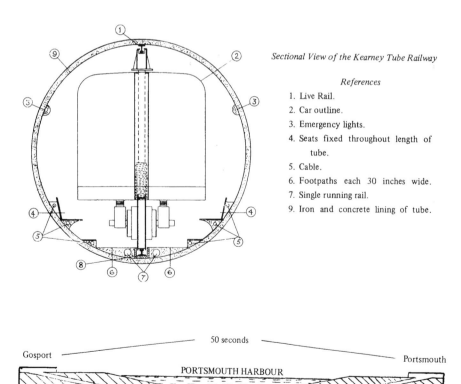

Sectional View of the Kearney Tube Railway

References

1. Live Rail.
2. Car outline.
3. Emergency lights.
4. Seats fixed throughout length of tube.
5. Cable.
6. Footpaths each 30 inches wide.
7. Single running rail.
9. Iron and concrete lining of tube.

Travel by Kearney High-Speed Tube Railway

A plan of the 'Kearney Tube' – the forerunner of one of the elements of today's Light Rapid Transit scheme.

109

Troops in Beach Street, Gosport, ready to embark on their landing craft to join the invasion fleet at Spithead.

Imperial War Museum, London

Troops at Beach Street, Gosport in 1944. Large numbers left this area for the invasion of Normandy.

Imperial War Museum, London

Chapter 8

SHORTER BY WATER

After the war, much time, effort and money had to be spent on repairing the devastation that had been wreaked upon Portsmouth and Gosport. The latter town centre had been particularly badly hit, and for a time the council directed its efforts towards the provision of housing at Rowner and Bridgemary to replace the many dwellings destroyed or irrevocably damaged within the town proper. Thus, for some years after the war, visitors to Gosport travelling across the Harbour found that the still-pretty Ferry Gardens served as a misleading prelude to a drab, battered and unlovely town centre.

In the Harbour, it was back to business as usual. All the boats except the veterans *Sir John Baker* and *Venus* returned to normal service. Although

Camper and Nicholson were busy building two new vessels, the *Ferry Princess* and a replacement for *Venus*, these proved to be of the now familiar design, albeit that they were equipped with triple-expansion steam engines instead of the old two-cylinder compounds. Meanwhile, a link with the remoter past of the ferry companies had been broken by the death in 1945 of eighty-nine-year-old Henry Redman, who as a boy had been apprenticed to his father who was a licensed waterman. Henry had eventually joined the 'New' company as long ago as 1884, and had skippered launches across the Harbour for over fifty years. Even in retirement, this grand old man had been unwilling to leave his beloved waterside – he spent a large part of each day in Ferry Gardens watching the familiar scene.

Gosport's Ferry Gardens in 1947. Anchored across the water is H.M.S. Vanguard, *while in the foreground an impressive array of Provincial buses await their next turn.*

A panoramic view of Gosport town and the ferries, c. 1947.

Portsmouth Harbour Ferry Co. Ltd.

Phone: Gosport 24551

PORTSMOUTH AND GOSPORT

Passenger, Motor-Cycle and Cycle Ferry Services

Portsmouth to Gosport 5.37½ a.m. to Midnight
Gosport to Portsmouth 5.30 a.m. to 11.50 p.m.
Peak Period 7½ minute Service. Off Peak 15 minute Service

Green Funnel Cruises

from

SOUTH PARADE PIER

CLARENCE PIER

and

GOSPORT PONTOON

by

"Gay Enterprise" and "Southsea Queen"

Write or phone for full particulars and fares
Private Hire available for Day and Evening Cruises
All vessels carry a D.T.I. Certificate

PRIVATE HIRE	**Gay Enterprise**	PRIVATE HIRE

Equipped for CONFERENCES, WEDDING RECEPTIONS, SOCIALS or any **PRIVATE OCCASION. Numbers up to 250 maximum. Modern decor throughout. Open and covered Dance Floor. Taped Recorded Music. First-Class Catering in tastefully styled Restaurant**

All cruises are subject to prevailing weather conditions, mechanical failure or any other cause beyond the Company's control

For information write: The Portsmouth Harbour Ferry Co. Ltd., South Street, Gosport, Hants. Telephone: Gosport 24551

Gosport Borough Council Town Guide Book, 1978

Isle of Wight Ferry leaving Portsmouth Harbour
(Photo Eric Stewart, Gosport)

Gosport & Portsmouth Ferry

FREQUENT SERVICES

From Gosport to Portsmouth, 5.30 a.m. to 11.50 p.m., for Harbour Station, Dockyard and all parts of Portsmouth

From Portsmouth to Gosport, 5.30 a.m. to midnight, for Fareham, Stokes Bay, Lee-on-Solent, Hill Head, etc.

Buses meet all boats   Passenger Fare 4d.

PRIVATE HIRE for Day, Half Day and Evening Trips Harbour Cruises, Day Trips to Cowes (I.W.) and Grand Circular Trips (Portsmouth-Cowes-Southampton-Portsmouth) from May to September, leaving Gosport, Clarence and South Parade Piers, Southsea, as advertised

Special Quotations for Coach and School Parties

The Portsmouth Harbour Ferry Co. Ltd.

Tel. Gosport 80067   FERRY GARDENS, GOSPORT, HANTS

Gosport Borough Council Town Guide Book, 1964

Advertisement from 1978 for the Green Funnel Cruises offered by the Ferry Company, featuring the Gay Enterprise, subsequently renamed.

Gosport and Portsmouth Ferry services in 1964. Note the fare of 4d in old money for crossing the Harbour – today's adult fare is £1.50.

J. Lawrence and Sons

Royal Reviews of the Fleet have always been popular attractions. This photograph shows the illuminated ships and firework display of the 1953 Coronation Review.

Gosport Society Collection

At the Coronation Review of 1953, the Royal Yacht Surprise *threads its way between H.M.S.* Vanguard *and the American cruiser* Baltimore.

Gosport Borough Council

A view down Gosport High Street in the early 1960s, long before pedestrianization and also before the covered bus station and the Harbour shops were built.

How the Portsmouth Hard area looked from the air in the 1960s, before the Hard Interchange and H.M.S. Warrior *made their appearances.*

For the time being, then, the ferry companies seemed content to carry on as before. But, in 1949, there appeared some sharp but constructive criticisms of the Harbour ferry services from an official source. This was the widely-publicised and very thorough Max Lock Report for Portsmouth and South-East Hampshire, which contained recommendations regarding the re-location of housing and industry in this area besides suggestions regarding improvements in travel facilities. Nearly forty years later, one could wish that there had been the money available as well as the inclination to implement more of the Report's conclusions!

As far as the ferries were concerned, the Report echoed some of the comments which daily travellers had been making for many years. While noting the efficiency, frequency and swiftness of the ferry services, the Report pointed out that the limited quayside accommodation for the boats prevented the provision of improved launches which could give adequate protection to passengers in bad weather. There was criticism of the delays and inconvenience caused by the distance between the bus stops and the ferry terminals, especially on the Portsea side where, the Report

recommended, the bus service should run alongside a newly-constructed covered-in ferry concourse. Much water was to flow through the Harbour before this particular suggestion became reality, as it was not until 1979 that the Hard Interchange was finally opened. On a similar theme, how many thousands of travellers from Gosport to the Isle of Wight must have wished, as they struggled with suitcases up the Portsmouth landing stage and then back in the opposite direction the length of the station platform, that a side entrance to the station could have been provided a little nearer to the pontoon.

How busy the ferries were in the late 1940s! The report lists 380 journeys each day, carrying some 24,000 passengers, with an evening peak between 4.30 and 6.30 daily of over 3000, when the boats were uncomfortably overcrowded. Since the Report had elsewhere proposed that about 17,000 people from the centre of Portsmouth might be re-housed in Gosport and Fareham, it also concluded that:

> serious consideration should be given to the building of a road tunnel from Gosport to Portsea.

The forlorn floating bridge Alexandra *lies partly submerged against the background of the new tower block flats on the Gosport side of the Harbour.*

It is rather ironic that it has taken a further half-century for this recommendation to have a chance of acceptance – but perhaps before too long we may see this hope come true thanks to the meticulously planned Light Rapid Transit scheme, which would certainly solve many of today's traffic problems. Meanwhile, even in 1949, getting to and fro in this area was difficult enough.

The antiquated floating bridge was carrying an average of 300 vehicles across the Harbour daily, 200 of which were private cars. 'The approaches on the Portsmouth side from Broad Street are inadequate,' grumbled the Report, which went on to criticise the floating bridge for not running in certain types of bad weather or particularly high tides. The long-term consideration of some form of tunnel was left for the councils of Gosport and Portsmouth to think about, with the warning that:

> improvement of the vehicular service should be undertaken at once, since this link vitally affects the commercial growth of Portsmouth and Gosport.

However big a splash in the Harbour the Report made at the time, most of those in authority, as far as travel facilities were concerned, were content to

let the ripples subside. Max Lock was followed by minimal change. One small but welcome concession to its findings was the appearance of a shelter over the Gosport pontoon in 1950. But all three companies were doing good business at the start of the new decade. The 'Old' and 'New' companies were carrying a huge number of passengers; and the floating bridge, too, was doing well, carrying over 80,000 vehicles a year across the Harbour. Thanks to rapid rises in the cost of petrol, many motorists found it cheaper to use the bridge. Among the passengers who boarded the old *Alexandra* floating bridge on 11 August 1951 were three men, Jack Law, Geoffrey Ashwell and Victor Jones, who were carrying some very unusual and heavy equipment with them. This proved to be a tape-recorder – an invention which at the time only a few people had heard of, let alone seen, together with its power supply. The men successfully recorded the noisy progress of the bridge across the Harbour from Broad Street, thus preserving the old monster's clanking and rattling for posterity on a record in the 'Argo' series of sounds of bygone transport.

Little did anyone realise in 1951 that within ten years the floating bridge would actually be an example of 'bygone transport'. A sad combination of circumstances combined to deal mortal blows to the company which had provided the only vehicular transport across the Harbour for over a century. The first misfortune occurred in 1952 when, just after the company had increased its fares for cars and commercial vehicles, the Government derationed petrol and brought down the price. Within a few months, twenty-eight firms, including such regular traders as Dyers, Fyffes, Whitbreads, Pinks, Vospers, McIlroys and the G.P.O. took the decision to drive round the Harbour rather than use the bridge. This produced a snowball effect. Soon the Portsea Island Co-operative Society and Brickwoods stopped using the bridge too. Such an alarming loss of revenue was bad enough, but now nature intervened in the shape of a sandbank near the Gosport slipway. This sandbank, caused by the peculiar nature of the tides in the Harbour, had slowly been building up until, in the years after 1950, at each new low tide the bridge was forced to come to a halt on the bank at a point too distant to offload its vehicles.

Receipts declined further when the company announced that the bridge would no longer be used in foggy conditions. At one time, the bridge had been the ONLY ferry that could operate, thanks to its regular chain-path, in safety in the fog – but thanks to radar, more vessels could now function in such conditions, thus increasing the danger of the bridge being hit by another boat. Really, the company was showing a commendable attitude towards water safety – but drivers, forced to crawl round the Harbour by road in severe fogs, such as the one which blanketed the area on 4 December 1955, did not see it that way.

The bridges were growing older and older. Repair costs, coal and insurance bills rose steeply. As the receipts dropped, the money was not available to make the necessary improvements. Grumbling grew about the stoppages, the breakdowns, the slippery ramps. The A.A. were reluctant to route anyone via the floating bridge in case of breakdowns. Desperately short of money, the company increased car tolls to half-a-crown in 1955; but petrol was still only 4/6 a gallon, having risen by only threepence since 1952. It was a vicious spiral; more and more drivers avoided the bridge and added to the Fareham congestion, while the company's losses grew greater.

Gosport Museum Collection

After ninety years of faithful service in the Harbour, an ignominious end for the floating bridge Alexandra *as she is broken up for scrap.*

A floating bridge comes in to land. Taken for granted for so many years, they disappeared from the local scene just at the time when road traffic started to grow alarmingly.

Faced with these dire difficulties, the company cast around for ideas to save the situation. They asked the local authority for assistance in dredging the sandbank, but without much success. They discussed the idea of selling their steam launches, and possibly using tank landing craft to replace the ancient bridges. But nothing came of any of these ideas. By 1959, both the *Alexandra* and *Duchess of York* were so badly in need of repair (it was estimated that over £20,000 was needed to make the service efficient again) that the ferry was suspended on 15 December. Most of the employees were laid off with the promise that they would have their jobs back again when the necessary repairs were complete. But they never were. Although originally the company had stated, 'There is no question of the floating bridge closing down', months passed and the service did not reappear.

Throughout 1960, arguments raged. Now that the floating bridge was no longer operating, many people realised just how useful it had been. Regular car-users of the bridge fumed. The local chambers of trade met to argue the different ways the Harbour might be crossed. Meanwhile, the floating bridge company had applied to the Ministry of Transport for financial assistance, without success. It was the end. The ninety-six-year-old *Alexandra* was sold to a scrap-dealer for a miserly £1250, chains, winches and all, while the

sixty-eight-year-old *Duchess of York* was broken up valueless.

It was widely expected that some alternative way of carrying vehicles across the Harbour would eventually appear. Certainly the matter was frequently discussed at Council and commercial levels on both sides of the water – but, as we all know, to no avail. Popular newspapers at this time were making much of the catchphrase 'the New Elizabethan Age', stressing the dynamic opportunities for all in post-austerity Britain. Gosport's 'New Elizabethans', noting the closure of the floating bridge and recalling the disappearance of passenger travel from Gosport railway station eight years earlier, must have wryly speculated that here, at least, travel facilities had been set back at least a century.

In the twenty-five years that have elapsed since the floating bridge disappeared, the provision of some form of vehicle ferry has often appeared to be tantalisingly just over the horizon. The joint committee set up by Portsmouth and Gosport Councils to consider the problem in 1963 went as far as to work out the details of a proposed new fixed ferry, on chains, for a basic cost of £520,000. Such a ferry, it was envisaged, would run a 24-hour-a-day service from Coldharbour to the Hard with boats that could carry 25 tons weight of vehicles and 500 passengers. Other suggestions were discussed, only to be similarly discarded later: a road tunnel, a swing bridge, a hovercraft service, a free-running car ferry and our old friend the 'Kearney Tube' the cost of which had now swollen to £2 million! But despite all the enthusiasm and hard work, the plans were left to gather dust on the shelves.

Complaints continued concerning the nuisance of driving through Fareham. 'It's a pain in the neck,' grumbled one reluctant van-driver, while a delivery man for a Portsmouth soft drinks firm said that it took him an hour to drive round to Gosport, particularly irritating if he had only one call to make. Some people pinned their hopes on the long-ago suggested new road south of Fareham. Others hoped that the versatility of that new vessel, the hovercraft, would solve the problem. But a spokesman for one of the hovercraft companies said that the congestion in the Harbour would prevent the high-speed operation essential to the economies of hover travel and, besides, the Harbour authorities would never grant permission for any really fast travel. The same authorities killed off any ideas for a bridge across the Harbour by insisting that such a construction would have to be at least 200 feet high to allow clearance for other ships.

Excitement was generated in 1972 with the news that British Rail were thinking about the possibility of using one of the Isle of Wight car ferries as a cross-Harbour vehicle transporter. Nothing came of this eventually, but the suggestion rekindled all the other schemes once again. Portsmouth City Council began discussing the Harbour tunnel idea again in the light of the ever-more pressing road problems and the major advances in tunnel construction methods. But as always, high costs proved to be the impenetrable barrier. The ideas keep resurfacing and as recently as 1983 a car ferry scheme emerged once more for discussion within Gosport Borough Council. The best hope must lie with the well-publicised and much-discussed Light Rapid Transit plan, introduced in 1992 by Hampshire County Council and given renewed impetus by its inclusion as one of the elements which make up the ongoing 'Renaissance of Portsmouth Harbour' scheme.

The collapse of the floating bridge company left the 'New' and 'Old' companies to provide the only public services for crossing the Harbour. In 1962 the two companies merged, as the new 'New' company changed its name to the Portsmouth Harbour Ferry Company and took over the 'Old' company. Since the two had been cooperating in the sharing of passengers and the pooling of

receipts for many years, it was a logical move. Soon the new company began to look into the possibility of a new type of ferry vessel, and in 1966 two of today's familiar apple-green-and-white boats, *Portsmouth Queen* and *Gosport Queen* began the first of many thousands of trips across the Harbour. Even now, these boats do not really look their age, and indeed were considered quite revolutionary in design and machinery when they were first constructed at Thornycroft's at Woolston. The almost identical vessels were both launched on the same day in April by Mrs P. D. Childs, wife of the chairman of the new Portsmouth Harbour Ferry Company, and Mrs A.E. Shier, wife of the then vice-chairman. The twin *Queens* came into use at once, replacing the five smaller vessels on the regular run, although an extra boat was maintained on standby for rush-hour services. Both of the new boats were very manoeuvrable, having 'Schottel' units which could turn through 360 degrees. Regular commuters were delighted. That increased comfort and protection from the winter weather, facilities which we all take for granted today, was very welcome for everyone in 1966, skippers and deck-hands included.

By the time the new ferry boats were established in the Harbour, striking alterations on the Gosport side had been made which certainly provided them with an up-to-date setting. Massive clearances and re-building gave the entrance to the town a face-lift. The new shops facing the water, the extensions to Ferry Gardens and, by 1972, the new bus station which finally replaced the old exposed stands, all played their part, but most spectacular of all were the sixteen-storey tower blocks with their unusual abstract murals. One gentleman who had not visited Gosport since before the war was horrified at the changes: 'We were aghast,' he wrote, 'no C and N slipways, where I remember the 'Js' in 1925 and 1930, but three sky-scrapers like multi-storeyed public lavatories where the "Thatched House" used to stand.' But then, changes never please everybody. Some Gosportonians disliked the removal of the older homes; others preferred the bright modern development.

As the 1960s drew to a close, amid the excitements of such events as Alec Rose's solo voyages across the Atlantic and round the world, the first discoveries of the *Mary Rose* relics and the Queen's visit to review the N.A.T.O. fleet, local commuters experienced a most unusual day in July 1968. Employees of the ferry company had organised a 24-hour strike; but what *The News* called 'the Dunkirk spirit' took over, and various assorted

As we have two Sponsors, namely, Mrs.P.D.Childs,
(Wife of the Chairman of the Portsmouth Harbour Ferry
Company), and Mrs.A.E.Shier, (Wife of the Vice Chairman
of the Portsmouth Harbour Ferry Co.Ltd.) who will name
the "Portsmouth Queen" and "Gosport Queen" respectively,
perhaps on the launching platform we will require some
slight modifications to the normal routine, as one expects
both ladies will want to have their hand on the launching
lever and so launch both ferries simultaneously.

An amusing comment regarding the preparations for the launch of the two new Queens *ferry boats in 1966.*

Portsmouth Harbour Ferry Co. Ltd

The Gosport approach to the ferry; to the right the bus station, completed in 1970.

Gosport Borough Council

Gosport Ferry Gardens in the 1970s, showing the old pontoon. Note the groups of children taking a dip! Swimming is banned in this dangerous area.

An aerial view of the entrance to the Harbour in the late 1960s. In the foreground is the Camber.

A 1980s view of Gosport Queen *in mid-harbour. To the far left is the approach to the extensive redevelopment.*

The Solent Enterprise *cruise ship glides past the old* Foudroyant, *once a familiar and well-loved 'wooden wall' moored for many years in the Harbour, and now at Hartlepool after refurbishment.*

Portsmouth Harbour Ferry Co. Ltd

Portsmouth Harbour Ferry Co. Ltd

Portsmouth pontoon and landing stage in the 1980s. Extreme left is Portsmouth Harbour station, which was opened in 1876 and has had several facelifts, particularly after suffering severe bomb damage during the Second World War.

On a calm, sunny day the 'Sealink' Isle of Wight car ferry makes stately progress as it passes Southsea Castle.

launches were assembled to enable regulars to cross the Harbour. Just to make things more difficult, on that particular day one of the flotation tanks beneath the Gosport pontoon was being replaced, rendering most of the landing-stage inaccessible for the boats. As a result, passengers had to use moored ferry boats as stepping stones! Although fewer people crossed the Harbour on that day, it seems that those who did quite enjoyed the unusual occasion.

The 1970s began brightly for the company with the introduction of a fine new vessel, originally christened *Gay Enterprise*. Equipped with a galley, dining room and dance-floor, she was designed mainly for cruising and social functions. It is a sad commentary on the decline of the English language that the company should have felt it

necessary to delete the word 'Gay' and rename her *Solent Enterprise*. All the same, the boat has been popular and successful. It was booked to capacity when it was used as a mobile grandstand for the starts of the Round the World Yacht Races and the Solent power boat events, to say nothing of those romantic cruises round local waters on warm summer evenings. For a brief time, another vessel, the *Southsea Queen*, also built with cruises in mind, was added to the fleet, but she was sold to the Hythe Ferry Company in 1978 for excursion work in Southampton water. Since then, the company, now known as Gosport Ferry Ltd, has celebrated the hundredth anniversary of its original parents' founding and under the slogan 'It's shorter by water' has continued to provide a vital service, with the boats carrying an estimated 2.7 million people round local waters each year.

Portsmouth Harbour Ferry Co. Ltd

The cruise vessel Solent Enterprise *about to pass the fifteenth-century Round Tower.*

Schoolchildren admire the Royal Yacht Britannia – *for so long a popular sight in the Harbour.*

Portsmouth Harbour Ferry Co. Ltd

For most local people, the event of the 1970s was the Queen's review of the fleet and her visit to Portsmouth to mark her Silver Jubilee. Throughout June 1977, excitement and discussion mounted as naval vessels began to gather in the Harbour and the Solent ready for the big day. Media attention was huge and plans were made by local authorities on a vast scale. It was imagined that there would be up to two million visitors in the area to see the Review. 75,000 parking spaces were arranged in Gosport and Portsmouth, one-way traffic systems were planned, massive stocks of souvenirs and food were laid up, and newspapers and local radio stations discussed schemes and suggestions as to how to avoid the expected traffic jams.

But when the time came, the crowds didn't come – at least, not in anything like the numbers anticipated. Why not? Local opinion suggested that the Jubilee Fleet Review had been oversold – the worrying forecasts of huge numbers of visitors almost certainly induced many would-be travellers to stay at home and watch the event on television instead. Nor did the weather encourage a holiday mood. The period of the Review was marked by

one of the coldest and gloomiest spells ever known in June. Indeed, a few days before the great event, when the first sightseers lined the shores to look at the ships drawn up in their lines, the weather produced a 'Nelson effect' – 'I see no ships' thanks to the hazy mist which shrouded the seascape.

The actual Review by the Queen went off without a hitch. Her Majesty, setting out on the Royal Yacht *Britannia* from the Harbour, was cheered by reasonably-sized crowds on the shores, and proceeded to review the fleet, impressed by the smart drill of almost 30,000 sailors who lined the 7 miles' length of the immaculately turned-out ships. Some people had made early claims to good vantage points, such as the two Polytechnic students who had camped out all night in the rain at the Round Tower, and the couple who had slept through the night in their car on Portsdown Hill. There was no doubting the enthusiasm of those who had turned out, but, as *The News* wrote:

> the expected tidal wave of traffic was little more than a steady trickle throughout the day.

So disappointing was the attendance that some traders pulled out of their seafront pitches and flag-sellers reported a sad lack of business, while the carefully worked-out 'Park and Ride' bus system in Portsmouth was hardly used. Would-be visitors on the day might also have been deterred by a dramatic but unfounded and untrue statement excitedly broadcast on Radio One that there were already a million people crowding into Southsea that very morning. Meanwhile, so cold was it, that hot drinks and food were much more in demand than ices, thus bringing useful profits to those caterers who had had the foresight to think of the British summer! Many local fishermen were able to enjoy a better catch than usual too, by offering tours round the ships in their open boats for up to £10 a time.

On the next day, the people's enthusiasm and warmth for the Queen's visit to Portsmouth and Southsea brought the week's events to a happy conclusion – even the sun made a brief appearance. Local loyalty and love was apparent to the Queen, who was heard to murmur, 'How friend-ly!' as the cheering crowds welcomed her near the Guildhall. But perhaps future organisers of mass celebrations should recall that events, however spectacular, can be 'sold' too much. That was certainly the view of the Portsmouth man who, at the conclusion of the Review, telephoned the police nerve centre in Kingston Crescent to say that he had stayed indoors for four days, and was it safe for him to come out now?

It was soon back to normal and, of course, for the most part, the regular ferries run smoothly and efficiently, but accidents and incidents will, of course, always catch the headlines. As with any other transport system, over the many years of operation the ferries have suffered scrapes and collisions; very occasionally, there have been injuries and in one or two cases, tragic deaths. In 1980, there was a fright for hundreds of passengers towards the end of rush-hour when, by a million-to one chance, both the *Queens* propellors were fouled by heavy-duty rope which had been left trailing from a dredger-hopper that was being towed into the Harbour. The stricken ferry boats and their passengers were left adrift in the middle of the Harbour until help arrived from a Royal Marine auxiliary boat and four smaller vessels from Butcher's Motor Launch Services which acted as emergency ferries. Sad to say, many passengers behaved badly, there was much pushing and shoving and many angry exchanges until the rescue problem had been safely sorted out.

A new aerial view of the entrance to the Harbour. In the foreground is Gosport with the remains of the eighteenth century ramparts and moats to the left by the tall flats. Haslar Creek is in the centre, with Fort Blockhouse and H.M.S. Dolphin to the right. The narrowest part of the Harbour between Blockhouse and the Round Tower (just visible) is about 200 yards wide.

Gosport Borough Council

Gosport Borough Council

On a perfect summer's day, a ferry approaches Gosport pontoon. The fully-enclosed structure was opened in 1983.

As nationwide inflation grew to alarming proportions in the late 1970s and early '80s, the ferry fares began to rise too. In 1979, a return ticket cost 20p. By the summer of 1980, it had risen to 28p. Early in 1981, the cost was 30p, and by June of the following year it was 36p. Meanwhile, there had been financial wrangling concerning both landing-stages. The ferry company had been paying a fixed annual sum to British Rail for the use and mainte-nance of the front of Portsea pontoon and half of the hinged gangway there since 1963, but in 1983 that agreement was due to expire. It was rumoured that British Rail was going to install a toll-gate and make a charge for every passenger who used it – but after long negotiations, local travellers breathed a sigh of relief when the ferry company agreed to acquire the Portsea pontoon from British Rail through a subsidiary company. At the same time, another potentially damaging and costly dispute between the ferry company and Gosport Borough came to a head. Ever since 1919, the ferry companies had paid a fixed sum to the Council for the use of Gosport landing stage. By 1981, the Council was complain-ing to Hampshire County Council that the cost of annual maintenance work on the pontoon was in the region of £60,000 – for which the company were only liable for a sum less than a thousand pounds. The County Council now introduced a Parliamentary Bill which sought to repeal the old Act relating to fixed charges. Again, luckily for the travelling public, a compromise was reached before things had gone too far. The ferry company agreed to make regular contributions towards the upkeep of the pontoon based on the number of people using the ferry.

As often happens, out of the gloomy clouds of financial wrangling came forth a shaft of bright sunlight in the shape of the Council's decision to build a fine new landing stage, giving increased comfort and protection for travellers and, hopeful-ly, reducing considerably maintenance costs. The sixty-year-old pontoon, however, stayed in the news a little longer. It was towed to Haslar Lake, and the company which had put it there hoped to be able to moor the old *Vadne* steam launch along-side it as part of a maritime heritage project. But these plans fell through. While suggestions within the Council for its use included the possibility of converting it into a fishing pier (this sport having been banned from the new landing stage), the new owners of the old jetty towed it round to Hardway where it was proposed that it should be used as a mooring for dinghies. The *Vadne* is currently under-going restoration.

Aerial view of 'D.E.R.A.' (Defence Evaluation Research Agency) inside Haslar Creek. In the left foreground are the remains of No.1 Ship Tank, built in 1884 and probably the world's first custom-built testing tank. No.2 Tank in the centre dates from 1932 and No.3 Tank was opened in 1960. Here nuclear submarines and oil rigs have been tested in model form. To the right of the picture is the Haslar Hospital complex, now facing an uncertain future after 250 years as a naval hospital.

Leisure sailors enjoying the Harbour.

129

H.M.S. Alliance *at the Submarine Museum in Gosport.*

Visiting schoolboys enjoy a sidelong view of H.M.S. Alliance.

Another attraction at the Submarine Musuem is the torpedo boat Holland I.

R.N. Submarine Museum, Gosport

Nomansland Fort. One of the four Palmerston sea forts, it was completed in 1880 at a cost of £242,487. During the Second World War all the forts were armed with anti-aircraft guns.

Spitsand Fort in tatty condition, showing the original platform on the right and the Second World War emergency ladder on the left.

In April 1982, the ferry commuters shared with the nation as a whole, a new and dramatic experience. For several months, speculation had been mounting as to the Argentinian government's intentions towards the British-owned Falkland Islands. Matters reached a head in the last days of March of that year when it became apparent that General Galtieri's troops were about to invade the Islands. On 5 April, a huge task force led by H.M.S. *Hermes* and H.M.S. *Invincible* sailed out of Portsmouth Harbour on the first leg of the 8000 mile journey to the South Atlantic. Once again in its 1000-year history the Harbour acted as a theatrical backdrop to a national event. For the people of the Harbour communities it was the kind of occasion with which their forebears would have been familiar. Few of those who witnessed the events of that day will forget the exuberance and emotion engendered by the awesome sight of those majestic ships whose crews had for so long rehearsed for just such an event.

Yet herein lay the supreme irony. On 2 April, 180 Dockyard men reporting for work had been handed their redundancy notices. They were the first casualties of a Ministry of Defence economy drive which would, during the next two years, result in the loss of over 3000 jobs. So it was that the task force of 28,000 men and 120 ships was assembed, converted, and stored by men who had been declared surplus to requirements, as were the ships they were asked to prepare for the conflict! H.M.S. *Hermes* was destined for the breakers' yards while H.M.S. *Invincible* was up for sale. It was a situation worthy of the plot of a Gilbert and Sullivan opera.

Sensing the angry mood in both Portsmouth and Gosport, *The News* organised a petition with 50,000 signatures with the slogan 'Keep the Fleet' which was sent to the Defence Secretary, John Nott. Maritime tradition and local pride soon asserted themselves, however, but there were mixed feelings among the actors in this cast of thousands. Amongst the ships' crews some reactions were predictable:

H.M.S. Hermes *approaching the Harbour on her return from the Falklands War 1982.*

Private Collection

Portsmouth

H.M.S. Hermes *returns to Portsmouth Harbour after the Falklands War.*

Private Collection

H.M.S. Illustrious *returns from the Falklands War in 1982.*

C.J.B. Photography

H.M.S. Invincible *entering the Harbour with assistance of tugs. In the background, the Gunwharf Quays site is under development, the City of Portsmouth stretches away beyond the top left of the picture, while Southsea Common is visible top right.*

Blueprint Communications

Gunwharf Quays site, just before the extensive redevelopment now in progress. At the bottom of the picture is H.M.S. Warrior and just above is Portsmouth Harbour railway station. Just above the helicopter pads is the entrance to the Camber, Old Portsmouth's commercial port, embarkation point for the Isle of Wight car ferries. Upper right is Old Portsmouth, Point and the Round and Square Towers. To the left of the picture are the old fortifications, Domus Dei garrison church and Portsmouth Cathedral.

C.J.B. Photography

The Gunwharf Quays site under development. This is to become a mixture of commercial, leisure and housing schemes. The original main gate can be seen, upper left; the gate is to be retained as a feature of the new development.

C.J.B. Photography

The Gunwharf Quays site looking across the Harbour to Gosport. Here is a magnificent study of the variety of vessels to be seen every day in the Harbour. Isle of Wight services are represented by the catamaran alongside the Harbour station and a car ferry anchored in mid-Harbour. Meanwhile a P & O boat heads up to the Continental Ferry Port, while a local ferry launch makes its way to Portsmouth. Lots of yachts can be seen in Gosport's marinas and just visible in the upper right of the picture is H.M.S. Warrior.

Private Collection

H.M.S. Warrior *is towed in the Harbour in 1987 following restoration in Hartlepool.*

Peter Titmuss Photography

One of the ferry companys's sightseeing Princess *boats of the 1980s gives holidaymakers a chance to enjoy a close-up waterside view of H.M.S.* Warrior.

I think I'm lucky to have the chance to face action. We're all trained up for this, although in your mind you know this is the real thing,

was the comment of a twenty-year-old able seaman. A rating was heard singing 'Don't cry for me, Argentina, I never loved you!' A more thoughtful view was voiced by an officer:

On the one side I can see the excitement of putting together all those things we've learnt over the years. But I don't think anyone would choose to fight if there was a satisfactory alternative.

An angry Naval wife made a political point:

I am bitter that the Government has allowed the Falkland Islands dispute to develop in this way.

And out in the Harbour, crowded on to the beaches, packed like sardines on the centuries-old Round Tower, crammed into the flower-decked Ferry Gardens, perched on the roofs of the Trinity Green tower blocks, the mass of local people cheered the ships and their crews, waved their flags, pointed their cameras, cried a little and pondered. . . Today as commuters on the Gosport side make their way down to the ferry, they pass the Falklands Gardens named in tribute to the men who lost their lives as a result of that encounter far away in the South Atlantic, but which started out here in Portsmouth Harbour.

One of the most colourful and exciting Harbour occasions was the return to Portsmouth of the massive iron-clad H.M.S. *Warrior* in June 1987. Escorted by ships of all shapes and sizes and watched by crowds on both sides of the Harbour, the 1860 warship took her proud place at a specially-built berth at the Hard where she has been a major tourist attraction ever since. What a contrast for H.M.S. *Warrior* – she had last been seen in the Harbour in 1929 when, after serving time as part of the floating torpedo school, she had been ignominiously towed away to Milford Haven to serve as a jetty for oil tankers. But now, thanks to a splendid restoration in Hartlepool, she had returned in superb fettle, a fine tribute to the skill of her Victorian engineers.

The approach to the Gosport Ferry landing stage through the colourful and airy gardens from which fine views of the Harbour can always be seen, the whole waterfront is being transformed with new walkways, street furniture and superb lighting.

H.M.S. Dryad

'Navy Days' programme cover for 1988. With the decline of the number of ships, these popular annual events have recently gone into abeyance, but the 1998 Festival of the Sea once again gave people the opportunity to examine Naval vessels.

A colourful forest of masts in the Harbour at the International Festival of the Sea in 1998.

International Festival of the Sea Ltd

This cartoon by the Gosport Ferry Company typifies the fun had by all at the Festival of the Sea in the Harbour.

The square-rigged Libertad *sails majestically into the Harbour at the beginning of the Festival of the Sea.*

International Festival of the Sea Ltd

The eighteenth century street market in the Dockyard, Festival of the Sea, 1998.

Private Collection

With a background of rigging almost reminiscent of the Harbour a century ago, the Polish three-masted barque Mir *takes a proud place at the Festival of the Sea.*

The Sedov, *the world's largest training ship, at the Festival of the Sea.*

The Argentinian square-rigger Libertad *made a striking appearance at the Festival of the Sea.*

Private Collection

55-K Class German U-boat 28, flanked by the Libertad *and H.M.S.* Warrior *at the Festival of the Sea.*

International Festival of the Sea Ltd

Private Collection

Here is the Matthew, *the Bristol-built replica of John Cabot's caravel which crossed the Atlantic 500 years ago. In August 1998, she sailed into the Harbour to provide an exciting attraction at the Festival of the Sea.*

Private Collection

The contraband carrying vessel and supportive hovercraft in the Royal Navy display at the Portsmouth International Festival of the Sea, August 1998.

Private Collection

Hovercraft Technical Service's 5-seat hovercraft and the Association of Search & Rescue Hovercraft's red craft participate in the Royal Navy display at the Festival of the Sea.

Hovercraft Technical Service's 5-seat hovercraft driven by managing director Brian Russell at the Festival of the Sea, 1998.

Hovercraft Technical Service's 5-seat craft returns to base, with a simulated engine fire, Festival of the Sea, 1998.

The colourful concluding ceremonies of the Festival of the Sea in August 1998.

International Festival of the Sea Ltd

The elegant tidal clock situated on the rocky boundary in front of the sea wall at Gosport, part of the extensive work being done to transform the waterfront as part of Gosport's Millennium Scheme.

So we approach the present day – and as we do, all around us we see and hear about the most spectacular changes in the entire history of the Harbour. When the Government outlined its plans to celebrate the Millennium by rewarding viable landmark projects with National Lottery cash, the initial foresight of a small group of local individuals led to the Gosport and Portsmouth Councils' bid to transform the waterfront by way of various ideas which eventually became known as the Renaissance of Portsmouth Harbour Millennium Scheme. Such a bold plan has involved lengthy and careful consideration and naturally the scheme has not been without its detractors, but in this first year of the new millennium locals and visitors alike are beginning to enjoy the first completed elements, such as the revamped Falkland Gardens with its new fountain, 'blue necklace' lighting scheme and its new pathways with the ingenious idea of bricks upon which local families can have their names engraved. Across the Harbour, the 'Festival Waterfront' at Gunwharf Quays will soon, hopefully, provide first-class leisure and shopping facilities. As well as providing a top-class waterfront which everyone can enjoy, the Renaissance scheme will certainly add to the area's potential for tourism and investment. After all this is a busy area. It has been estimated that three million passengers use

the channel ferries each year, together with two million crossing the Solent and there are well over 60,000 movements of vessels passing through the Harbour. If these visitors enjoy the ambience of a revitalised, vigorous and smart waterscape, they are more likely to return. The same is true of investors and events' organisers. Already the Harbour has been granted the 2001 International Festival of the Sea, which, assuming the Renaissance Scheme is completed, should even surpass the magnificent earlier version of the event in August 1998 when good crowds enjoyed the 700 vessels which attended together with the entertainments over the Bank Holiday.

It is true, as we have tried to show in this book, the Harbour and its towns have a worthy and fascinating heritage. But without nourishment and care, things will decay. Within all our living memories, the Harbour has come to influence our lives. In a practical sense, the ferries – and maybe in the not-so-distant future, the Light Rapid Transit system under the Harbour – serve us as a means of work and leisure. On another level, the crossing links together not simply two historic communities but is a commentary on the daily lives of people past, present and future. We look forward to a truly world-class waterfront for the new millennium.

One of the attractive Millennium Mosaics on Gosport's waterfront. The stone commemorating the D-Day embarkations of 1944 can also be seen.

The Millennium Project, including the controversial Tower.

INDEX

SOURCES

1. *The Gosport Ferry – the Centenary of the Portsmouth Harbour Ferry Company PLC 1883-1983*, by P.D. Childs O.B.E., J.P.

2. *The Port of Portsmouth Floating Bridge 1838-1961*, by Mrs J. Finch, 1971.

3. *Solent Passages and their Steamers 1820-1981*, by Ken Davies. Published by the Isle of Wight County Press, 1982.

4. *Roads, Rails and Ferries of the Solent Area 1919-1969*, by D. Fereday Glenn. Published by Ian Allan Ltd, 1980.

5. *Transports of Delight*, by Ron Brown. Published by Milestone Publications, 1982.

6. *The Story of Gosport*, by Dr L.F.W. White. Published by W.H. Barrell, 1964.

7. *Great Years in Yachting*, by John Nicholson. Published by the Nautical Publishing Company, 1970.

8. *Historic Sketches of Gosport, Alverstoke and Rowner*, by Arthur A. Walford. Published by Walford & Sons, 1887.

9. *Portsmouth*, by Alan Balfour. Published by Studio Vista, 1970.

10. *The Solent Way*, by Barry Shurlock. Published by Hampshire County Council, 1984.

11. *Change into Uniform*, by Helen Long. Published by Terence Dalton, 1978.

12. *Book of Portsmouth*, by James Cramer. Published by Barracuda Books, 1985.

13. *Illustrated History of Portsmouth*, by William G. Gates. Published by Charpentier & Co., 1900.

14. *Guide to Portsmouth, Southsea, Anglesey and Hayling Island*, by W.H. Charpentier. Published by Charpentier & Co., 1900.

15. *Gosport Records, Nos. 1, 2, 5, 6, 7, 13, 14, 15, 17*. Published by the Gosport Society.

16. *Gosport Goes To War*, by Lesley Burton. Published by the Gosport Society, 1981.

17. *Gosport 1922*, by Lesley Burton. Published by the Gosport Society, 1982.

18. *The Diary of a Portsmouth Dockyard Worker*, by John Field, B.A. – an article in the Portsmouth Archives Review Vol. 3. Published by Portsmouth City Records Office, 1978.

19. *Portsmouth Railways*, by Edwin Course, B.Sc.(Econ.), Ph.D., AMinstT. (Portsmouth Papers 6). Published by Portsmouth City Council, 1969.

20. *The Siege of Portsmouth in the Civil War*, by John Webb, M.A., F.R.Hist.S. (Portsmouth Papers 7).
Published by Portsmouth City Council, 1969.

21. *A History of Portsmouth Theatres*, by H. Sargeant F.L.A. (Portsmouth Papers 13).
Published by Portsmouth City Council, 1971.

22. *Portsmouth – as others have seen it, Part I*, by Margaret J. Hoad, M.A. (Portsmouth Papers 15). Published by Portsmouth City Council, 1972.

23. *Portsmouth – as others have seen it, Part II*, by Margaret J. Hoad, M.A. (Portsmouth Papers 20). Published by Portsmouth City Council, 1973.

24. *Early Man in Portsmouth and South-East Hampshire*, by David J. Rudkin, B.A., A.M.A. (Portsmouth Papers 31). Published by Portsmouth City Council.

25. *Scheme for the Improvement of Communications between Portsmouth and Gosport*.
Published by William Pink & Sons, 1894.

26. *Harbours of the Solent*, by John Scott-Hughes. Published by Christopher Johnson, 1956.

27. *Portsmouth From the Air*, by Anthony Triggs. Published by Phillimore & Co. Ltd., 1995.

28. *Voyage Around The Solent With Solent Enterprise – Video*. Published by Gosport Ferry Ltd., 1999.

29. The *Hampshire Telegraph*, 1799 onwards. The *Evening News*, 1919 onwards (later *The News*). *Hampshire* magazine, 1967 onwards. *Model Engineer* magazine, June 1956. *Pink's Pictorial* magazine, 1898. The *Gentleman's Magazine*, November 1802.